Going to Zero 2019

Student Projects for Environmental Control Systems
Spring Semester of 2019

Cal Poly Pomona University
Department of Architecture
College of Environmental Design

Professor
Pablo La Roche

Instructional Assistant
Jake Chevrier

Graphic Design
Liliana Perez

Images are from 2030 Palette, HEED, Climate Consultant and the students.

Edited by

Pablo La Roche PhD
Professor

All rights reserved by student team authors who are solely responsible for their content.

Table of Contents

Introduction	5
The Approach	6
The Course	7
Assignment	8
Process	10
Houses and Team Members	11
Going to Zero Houses	16

Introduction

The production of the energy used to operate buildings contributes a significant amount of Greenhouse Gases to the atmosphere. Commercial and residential buildings use almost 40% of the primary energy and approximately 70% of the electricity in the United States (EIA 2005).

The world reached a very important consensus in 2015 under the Paris Agreement – to limit global average temperature increase to "well below 2°C and to drive efforts to limit the temperature increase even further to 1.5°C above pre-industrial levels." It is impossible to achieve these necessary reductions in anthropogenic emissions without implementing significant reductions in the building sector. Even though this reduction in energy use can be achieved using current technologies, it requires a new set of skills and a transformation in how we think about buildings and how we design and produce them. The education needed for this transformation must begin early in architecture school.

All architects must know how to design Zero Net Energy (ZNE) buildings and Zero Net Carbon (ZNC) buildings. Zero Net Energy buildings will have lower operating costs and a reduced impact on climate change. In California, all new residential buildings must be ZNE by 2020 and all new commercial buildings by 2030. Students in this class are in the second-year undergraduate program or in the first-year graduate program at Cal Poly Pomona. These students will be designing the zero energy buildings that we need tomorrow.

Architects and engineers must work together to achieve zero net energy buildings. Architects usually have responsibility in the design of the envelope (form and materials) while mechanical engineers are responsible for the mechanical systems that cool and heat the building. True integrated sustainable design is achievable working together. This project emphasizes the student's role as a "designer" of buildings that provide comfort with zero net energy.

The Approach

To reduce anthropogenic impact on climate change architecture schools must provide a more comprehensive sustainable design education to ALL architecture students. This education includes concepts and tools. Students must have the knowledge to implement the appropriate measures to reduce the building emissions, while also having the knowledge to use appropriate tools to test ideas, typically using building simulation tools. However, when architecture students are introduced to energy modeling, it is only in graduate or advanced undergraduate seminars, and when they are introduced to the design of Zero Net Energy, low carbon buildings it is only in upper division studios. These courses are not required, and only a small fraction of architecture students in some universities are able to take them. This is not enough. To reduce our impact on climate change we must introduce these concepts and tools to ALL architecture students. A good place to do this is in a required lecture course that all students must take.

Architecture students typically learn by implementing concepts taught in lecture courses in their design projects, typically in studios. However, it is also possible to implement design-oriented exercises directly in lecture courses. This, however, is a challenge due to the large number of students in these courses. The author has tested two approaches to implement sustainability oriented design exercises in lecture courses. The first approach is analog. Students built test cells which had to maintain comfortable conditions using only passive strategies. This approach has the advantage that students learn by building with their hands, feeling the forces of the sun and nature with their bodies. In the second approach, which is implemented in this course, and collected in this book, students design a zero net energy & zero net carbon building using energy modeling software and other digital tools.

There is a limit to the number of variables that a designer can consider simultaneously to solve a problem. In these exercises the number of variables that students must consider is reduced, with an emphasis on energy, allowing the students to think more about one issue.

Intelligent use of energy, especially coming from the sun and the wind, should play a major role in a sustainable building. Students should learn the basics of building physics and understand the relationship between the building envelope and energy. Special emphasis is placed on how energy can move through the envelope by conduction, convection and radiation. It is more important to understand the concepts, once these are clear it is possible to learn how to use different tools to evaluate their implementation. Students should learn how to use digital and analog tools as appropriate. The precision of design tools is generally inversely proportional to their ease of use. Easy to use tools, with sufficient precision, are especially useful in the initial stages of the design process. It is not enough to know how to use the software, it is also important to know how to use it correctly to test concepts.

The Course

ARC3310 is the first of two required Environmental Control System courses at Cal Poly Pomona University. All second-year undergraduate students and first year graduate students are required to take this class. The course lasts fifteen weeks and includes six topics:

1. Psychrometrics and thermal comfort
2. Site, climate and architecture
3. Solar geometry
4. Energy and buildings: passive heating and cooling, renewable energy and solar active heating.
5. Mechanical heating and cooling
6. Daylight

The course was conducted in both lecture and seminar/lab formats. It involves theory, practical applications, calculations, and appropriate hands-on experiments with building performance modeling tools. Topics are explained in lectures, practiced in the labs and integrated into the design process through the Net Zero Energy Project. Lectures introduce the concepts which are also connected to the readings. There is more emphasis in the lectures and laboratory projects in the first half of the quarter, shifting to implementation of concepts in the Net Zero Energy project in the second part of the course. An active learning program was implemented to engage students in the class for discussion of the AIA 2030 and lecture topics. The AIA+2030 Online Series Certificate Program is linked to the lectures and was required viewing. The courses are based on the AIA+2030 Professional Series, which was created by AIA Seattle and Architecture 2030, with support from the City of Seattle and Northwest Energy Efficiency Alliance. AIA provided free access to the students for the duration of the semester and even though the certificates were not required a majority of the students took the quizzes and received certificates.

Assignment

Los Angeles is home to many emblematic twentieth-century houses, many of which have tried to respond to the climate and harmonize with nature using technology that allowed for a greater indoor-outdoor flow and an emphasis on outdoor living. Many of the homes dating from the 1950s were built at a time when a new lifestyle was coming of age, when users sought healthful, well-lit homes built by industries that the end of the war had left idle. Architects tried to integrate with nature using materials such as glass and steel in the new designs. Specialized journals such as Arts and Architecture, particularly under the Case Study House Program undertaken in 1945 encouraged and documented this new attitude. However, even though these homes understood the importance of climate they did not have to respond to an energy code and lacked many of the basic responses that current homes now have. Students selected one of five well-known mid-century homes in Los Angeles, analyzed it and then implemented design measures to achieve zero net energy and zero net carbon performance. The houses that they could use are:

1. King's Road House by Rudolf Schindler
2. VDL house by Richard Neutra
3. Eames House by Charles and Ray Eames
4. Case Study House 22 by Pierre Koenig
5. Kappe House by Ray Kappe

Students first analyzed their projects as they were originally designed, comparing their performance with that of a California Energy Code compliant building (Title 24-2013). They then made all necessary modifications to improve building performance, beyond code, and achieve net zero energy. In this process students used a climate analysis tool (Climate Consultant) and an energy modeling software (HEED). Both were developed by UCLA's energy design tools group and are available for free on their website.

http://www.energy-design-tools.aud.ucla.edu/

The general goal of the course is to introduce the basic concepts in sustainable architectural design, with an emphasis on energy. The specific goal of this assignment is to provide a hands-on opportunity to implement the concepts taught in class and to learn by doing. The project introduced students to the process of designing zero net energy buildings with energy modeling as an important part of the process. There were 115 students in the course, organized in teams of 5 students each and developed over the second half of the semester.

All projects are included in this publication. The boards have been shrunk to 25% of their original size, maintaining the spirit of the design, however with a smaller text. Time was a constraint and in all projects there is still room for improvement. However, the student work demonstrates that it is possible to introduce the basics of energy modeling and zero net energy design in a large lecture course.

Process

The United States Department of Energy DOE (2015) states that a Zero Energy Building is an energy-efficient building where, on a source energy basis, the actual annual delivered energy is less than or equal to the on-site renewable exported energy. A zero-net energy (ZNE) building is a very energy efficient building that produces enough renewable energy to meet its own annual energy consumption requirements, reducing the use of non-renewable energy in the building sector. Typically, a Zero Net Energy Building is connected to the electrical grid and uses energy from the grid when renewable energy produced on site is not enough to meet its needs, sending surplus energy to the grid when it generates more energy than it uses. In a ZNE building the grid acts as the battery for storage.

Depending on where the energy is measured, a Zero Net Energy building can be Site Zero Energy or Source Zero Energy. A source ZNE building produces as much energy as it uses as measured at the source, where this energy is produced. A site ZNE building produces as much energy as it uses, when accounted for at the site where the building is located. The main advantage of using the site zero net energy definition is that it is easy to understand and measure, typically using meters (electric and gas). For this project the site zero net energy definition is used.

A Zero Net Carbon, ZNC building is defined by Architecture 2030 as a highly energy efficient building that produces on-site, or procures, enough carbon-free renewable energy to meet annual building energy consumption. A ZNC building will also be a ZNE building.

A carbon neutral building is one in which total emissions are equal to zero (Carbon Neutral Architectural Design 2017). This carbon neutrality is accomplished by reducing the emissions in the different categories as much as possible and then offsetting the emissions with renewable sources. If only emissions from energy are considered, then the equation below is used in which the emissions from non-renewable energy are offset by the generation of renewable energy (or partially by carbon offsets).

$$0 >= T_{be} = O_e - R_s$$

Where
T_{be} = total building emissions
O_e = operation emissions (energy)
R_s = Renewable Strategies

If, in addition to energy, water, waste and construction are also considered, then the emissions from these must be added to the emissions from energy and the equation below is used. In this case the emissions offset from the production of renewable energy must offset all the other emissions and the building is net positive for energy though still net zero for carbon.

$$0 >= T_{be} = O_e + C_e + W_e + W_a - R_s$$

Where
Tbe = total building emissions
Oe = operation emissions (energy)
Ce = construction emissions
We = water emissions
Wa = waste emissions
Rs = Renewable Strategies

For this course students focused on emissions from the operation of the building and which are calculated by HEED.

This exercise had the following learning objectives:

a) Understand the effects of climate on building thermal performance.
b) Understand how to design a building adapted to climate using weather files and climate analysis software.
c) Determine the impact of design strategies such as form and orientation, window to wall ratio, shading and building materials & strategies on energy use and emissions.
g) Determine the most effective design strategies for residential buildings in selected climates.
h) Understand the basic principles of zero net energy building design.

To achieve these learning objectives the students followed a process divided in three basic steps: First they analyzed climate and its relationship with passive strategies, then they analyzed the homes as originally designed, and finally they proposed strategies to achieve zero net energy in the original homes.

Step 1: Climate Analysis

Climate analysis allowed the students to better understand the relationship of the buildings with the environment around them and the effect of climate on buildings so that they could select the most appropriate bioclimatic design strategies. Climate Consultant is a simple to use, graphic-based computer program that helps users understand local climate. It uses annual 8760-hour EPW format climate data and translates this raw climate data into graphic displays, also providing design guidelines and suggestions. Many of these guidelines include a link to the 2030 Palette, which allows the students to learn from built examples and better understand the strategies that can be implemented. The climate analysis also helped define the overheated period during which the buildings require shade, which also had to respond to each orientation and climate. Students used the building bioclimatic chart to determine effective climate responsive design strategies and then used the 2030 palette to see examples of buildings that implemented these strategies.

Step 2: Analysis of the Original Building

Analyzing the building in its original state allowed the students to understand the climate responsive design strategies that the original architects had implemented many years ago: what worked and what did not work. Students were asked to look at the site, the building layout and massing, the envelope, and solar and wind control strategies, all this using energy modeling tools and metrics such as Energy Use Intensity (EUI). Students were asked to illustrate the original strategies with drawings, photographs, diagrams and calculations.

Step 3: Design to Zero
After understanding how the buildings worked, the students proposed design strategies to improve performance and achieve net zero energy. These strategies were tested systematically, one at a time, using HEED, comparing results to determine their individual effect on energy, expenses and carbon. Strategies included adding insulation in the walls, upgrading to higher performing windows, adding or extending overhangs or fins for shading, and design modifications that affected the form and enclosure. Performance metrics were an important part of the "design to zero" process and students had to compare each option with the original house as it was being tested. Special emphasis was placed on Energy Use Intensity (EUI) and Carbon Intensity as guiding metrics. Results were also reported in drawings, diagrams, sections, perspectives, and renderings that included technical information as appropriate (e.g. U value and SHGC). A before and after diagram with strategies and metrics comparing the original and proposed buildings was encouraged.

Houses and Team Members

Case Study House 22
by Pierre Koenig

Team 1
- Kim Tran
- Wenbin Jiang
- Janis Liu
- Efrain Vargas
- Sophia Convert - Cuevas

Team 2
- Natalie Chug
- Jamie Guevara
- Ulysses Hernandez
- Jessica Lam

Team 3
- Junhong Wen
- Vi Vo
- Vivian Liao - Zeng
- Apinya Sangrugee
- Ying Gao

Team 4
- Caitlin Mouri
- Elizabeth Chan
- Melissa Gracia
- Michel Williams
- Eric Martinez
- Jose Martinez

Team 5
- Ghazi Ghazi
- Jose Nunez
- Francisco Reyes Sanchez
- Isaiah Rojas
- Victor Rodriguez

Eames House
by Charles and Ray Eames

Team 6
- Sharifeh Abdallah
- Sarineh Nahapedsiraki
- Alenoosh Mardroosian
- Nerjis G. Kalkan Almonte
- Natalie Simba

Team 7
- Maribel Ruiz
- Yeganeh Malouhi
- Nauryzbek Naurbekov
- Natalie Valle
- Kristin Lorentzen

Team 8
- Frank Ruedas
- Dung Quoc Dinh
- Rita Jirjees
- Kimberly Carlisle
- Noah Lemus

Team 9
- Kristal Audish
- Upavee Amarasinghe
- Jared Pablo
- Krissandra Perez
- Daniela Pomalaza

Team 10
- Joshua Ryan
- Olivia Nilges
- Heather Gallacher
- Alex Gonzalez
- Emane Henderson

Kappe House
by Ray Kappe

Team 11
- Noah Mora
- Trevor Kubo
- Michael Joya
- Vincent Nguyen

Team 12
- Addy Holenstein
- Sarra Starbird
- Roman Huante
- Zoe Zimmerliny
- Ashley Morales

Team 13
- Peyra Rodriguez
- Valeria Redekosky
- Brarolice Reza
- Marc Mendez
- Ashy Saucedo

Team 14
- Sidra Issa
- Alex Menjivar
- Jaylene Sanchez
- Christian Serrano
- Anne Marie Jao

Houses and Team Members

King's Road House
by Rudolf Schindler

Team 15
    Noah Lum
    Lorenzo Tayag
    Ivanah Sagabaen Palagarias
    Yaozhen Liu
    Daniel Alejandro Aguilera

Team 16
    Carl Arnesto
    Daniel Vasquez
    Sandee Deogaygay
    Khoi Van
    Team members

Team 17
    Brian Caballero
    Juan Garcia
    Michael Hernandez
    Emanuel Cardenas
    Ivonne Murillo

Team 18
    Mahshid Safarian
    Diarra Seck
    Adrian Martinez
    Rana Matinsefat
    Anita Dehmoobad
    Haniyeh Poshtareh

VDL House
by Richard Neutra

Team 19
    Jose Arce
    Cristian Cedillo
    Alondra Delgado
    Justina Atalla
    Alexis Alicea

Team 20
    Khanh Dinh
    Toan Nguyen
    Eduardo De La Rosa
    Huda Alhassan
    George Jang

Team 21
    Noel Cordero
    Ulysses Ojeda
    Gabriella Torres
    Cho Zin Theint
    Daniela Vargas

Team 22
    Enrique Mora
    Jorge Torres
    Robert Ambriz
    Alex Tapia
    Cynthia Martinez

Team 23
    Josue Navarro
    Hannah Doan
    Gabriela Martinez
    Ruth Morales
    Nayeon Kim

Case Study House 22
City, CA | Architect: Pierre Koenig

Case Study House 22
City, CA | Architect: Pierre Koenig
Group 1: Kim Tran, Wenbin Jiang, Janis Liu, Efrain Vargas, Sophia Convert - Cuevas

Case Study House 22 is located in Los Angeles, which is in climate zone 9. It has an average annual temperature of about 62 degrees fahrenheit. Summer temperatures range from 64 to 84 degrees fahrenheit. Winter temperatures range from 8 to 66 degrees fahrenheit, as indicated on the temperature range chart and timetable plot. Los Angeles is located at 34.15 degrees north latitude and 118.5 degrees west longitude, according to the weather file.

The psychrometric chart shows that the average temperature for climate zone 9 is slightly below comfort zone, with some temperature periods that are hotter. According to the charts, only 12.1% of the time is within the comfort zone. Therefore, this area would benefit from more internal heat gain.

The sun-shading charts show that from June to October, the area is exposed to 1193 hours of direct sun (generally 9 a.m to 6 p.m) without any shading device installed. During the winter-spring months, it is warm/ hot from April to June at 9 a.m to 4 p.m. It is more cool/cold, so not much shading is necessary.

The timetable pot and temperature range show that the dry-bulb temperature for Los Angeles. The hotter temperatures occur generally around June and end in October from 8 a.m to 8 p.m, whereas the temperatures during cooler months are around October to June from 12 p.m to 4 p.m. Relative humidity for climate zone 9 is high during January and December, and also during July and September. The triple pane windows insulate and keep the house warm during the winter, but can be slid open during the summer to allow air flow throughout. Also, the open floor plan ensures there is little obstruction so that wind can flow easily within. [Glass type: triple pane advanced low-e insulating glass with argon^2 (1⅜" triple pane insulating glass panels with foam insulation: U-Factor: 0.22, SHGC: 0.23, VLT: 0.40, CR: 61)

Strategically placed trees grow thick leaves in the warmer months, thus creating protection from direct sunlight. During the winter time, they shed their leaves and the house receives more sunlight, keeping it warm during cooler months. Intercepting sunlight before it reaches the walls and glazing of a building dramatically reduces the amount of heat entering that building. External shading devices can reduce solar heat gain through glazing by up to 80%. By designing shading devices according to the sun's seasonal path, both summer shading and winter solar gain can be achieved in climates with seasonal variations.

The advantages of installing louver windows includes the free passage of air through the house, and sufficient light for the interior even when closed. Due to the size of the window, it would not obstruct natural ventilation that occurs while providing protection against excessive daylight and glare inside the house. Louvers is energy efficient, as it used the natural ventilation to reduce heating and cooling cost. Additionally, adjustable shading devices such as louver can be angled to control seasonal temperature variations or user control during unusually warm or cool periods. The Stahl house is placed on a hill and receives a lot of sunlight. The house will require significantly less energy with solar panels placed on the roof. The trees lose their leaves during the winter time, ensuring that the panels will still work efficiently to provide energy for the house.

RESPONSE TO CLIMATE

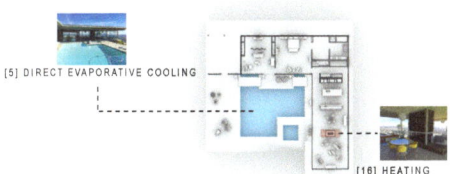

[5] DIRECT EVAPORATIVE COOLING

[16] HEATING

CASE 22

CASE STUDY HOUSE 22
(STAHL HOUSE)

Janis Liu, Kim Tran, Effrain Vargas, Wenbin Jiang, Sophia Covert-Cuevas

CLIMATE ANALYSIS

RESPONSE TO CLIMATE

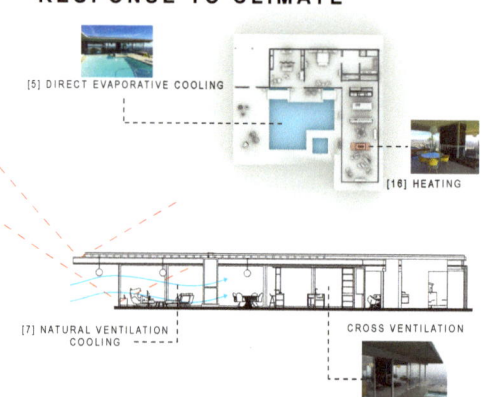

[5] DIRECT EVAPORATIVE COOLING
[16] HEATING
[7] NATURAL VENTILATION COOLING
CROSS VENTILATION

EXISTING SHADE

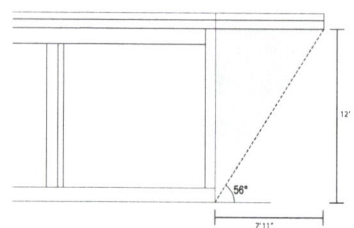

OP = 7'11"

DEPTH = HEIGHT/TAN (VSA)
DEPTH = 7'11" HEIGHT = 12'
7.916' = 12'/TAN (VSA)
7.916' × TAN (VSA) = 12'
TAN (VSA) = 12'/7.916'
TAN (VSA) = 1.516
VSA = TAN^-1(1.516) = 56.6 DEGREES

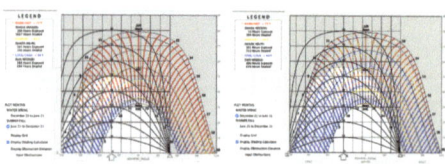

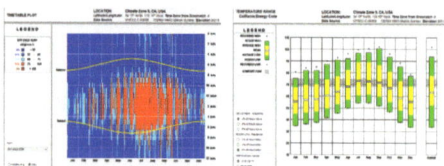

BIOCLIMATIC STRATEGIES

OVERHEATED & UNDERHEATED PERIODS

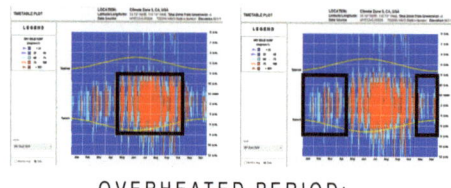

OVERHEATED PERIOD:
MAY TO OCTOBER:
7:30 AM - 6 PM

UNDERHEATED PERIOD:
NOVEMBER TO APRIL:
12 PM - 4 PM

Cantilever Sketch

Floor Plan

Cantilever

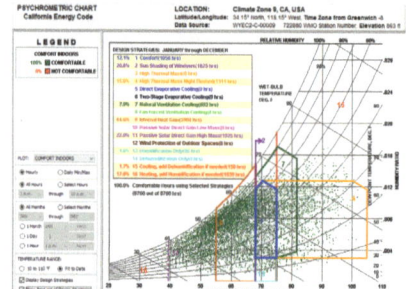

- SUN SHADING OF WINDOWS (20.8%)
- INTERNAL HEAT GAIN (44.6%)
- PASSIVE SOLAR DIRECT GAIN HIGH MASS (22.0%)

2030 PALETTE STRATEGIES

CROSS VENTILATION   SOLAR SHADING   DOUBLE ROOF

JOSEY PAVILLION

TUTERE HOUSE

KANGAROO VALLEY HOUSE

CASE STUDY HOUSE 22
(STAHL HOUSE)

Janis Liu, Kim Tran, Effrain Vargas, Wenbin Jiang, Sophia Covert-Cuevas

IMPROVED SHADE ANALYSIS

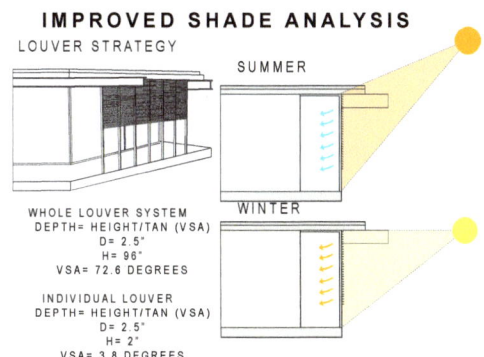

LOUVER STRATEGY

SUMMER
WINTER

WHOLE LOUVER SYSTEM
DEPTH = HEIGHT/TAN (VSA)
D = 2.5"
H = 96"
VSA = 72.6 DEGREES

INDIVIDUAL LOUVER
DEPTH = HEIGHT/TAN (VSA)
D = 2.5"
H = 2"
VSA = 3.8 DEGREES

PROPOSED STRATEGIES
ZERO NET ENERGY HOME

1. TRIPLE PANE WINDOWS
2. DECIDUOUS TREES
3. LOUVERS
4. SOLAR PANELS

PERFORMANCE METRICS

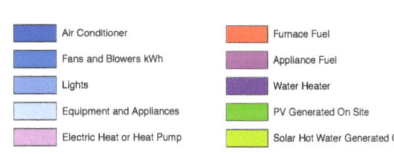

- Air Conditioner
- Fans and Blowers kWh
- Lights
- Equipment and Appliances
- Electric Heat or Heat Pump
- Furnace Fuel
- Appliance Fuel
- Water Heater
- PV Generated On Site
- Solar Hot Water Generated On Site

Annual Cost:
Originally: $2676.78
Proposed: -$388.64

Site EUI:
Originally: 57.39 kBTU/sqft
Proposed: -0.38 kBTU/sqft

Site Energy:
Originally: 41848.51 kWH
Proposed: 16787.29 kWH

CO_2 Site Production:
Originally: 17724.18 lbs
Proposed: 10371.43 lbs

CLIMATE RESPONSIVE STRATEGIES

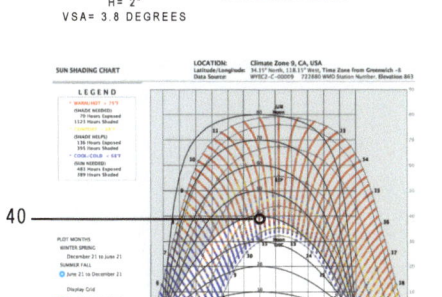

SLOT, DOOR, JAMB, SILICONE WEATHER STRIPPING, ATTACHED CHANNEL, GLIDE, FREE CHANNEL, DOOR, SILICONE SWEEP, SUN

TREES PLANTED AROUND THE OUTDOOR SPACE CREATES MORE SHADE THROUGHOUT THE DAY

U-FACTOR 0.22
SHGC 0.23
VLT 0.40
CR 61

- DOOR TYPE: PREMIUM VINYL SLIDING PATIO DOOR PELLA® 350 SERIES
- GLASS TYPE: TRIPLE PANE ADVANCED LOW-E INSULATING GLASS WITH ARGON^2 (1-3/8" TRIPLE-PANE INSULATING GLASS)

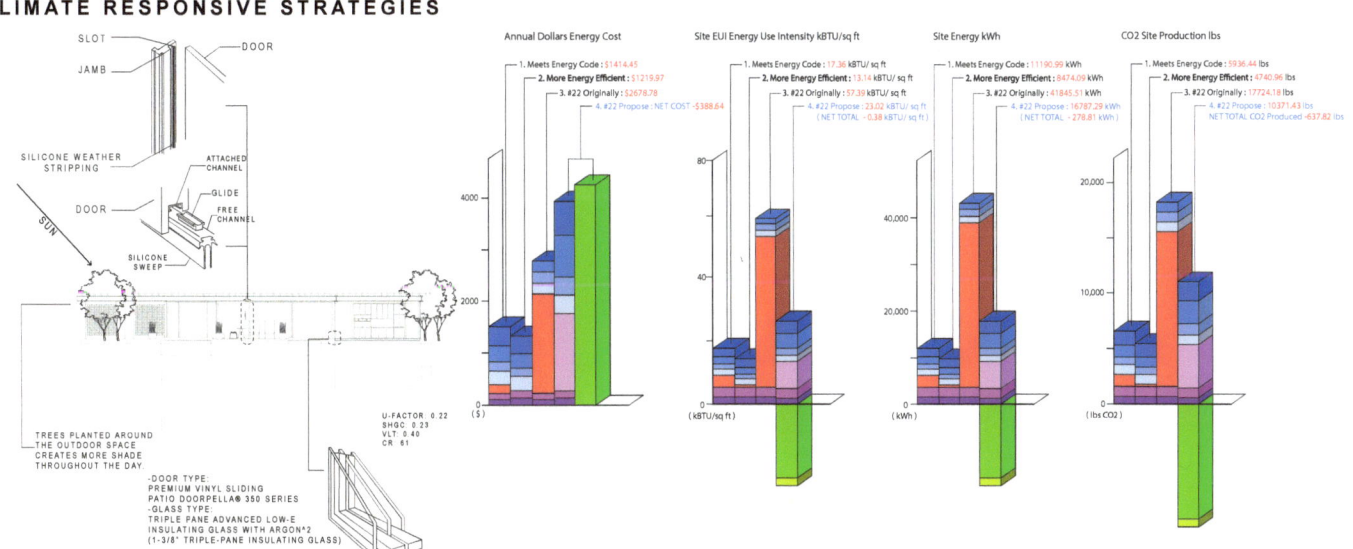

Case Study House 22
City, CA | Architect: Pierre Koenig
Group 2: Natalie Chug, Jamie Guevara, Ulysses Hernandez, Jessica Lam

Two of the main sustainable strategies in the Case Study House 22, Stahl House, are natural lighting and cross ventilation. The house has a south facing window with an overhang, which allows for direct natural lighting and heating during the winter time. This has a Vertical Shadow Angle of 59 degrees. The roof has multiple overhangs at the border of the house, therefore it provides shade for the interior during the hot summer months when the sun is higher in the sky. The house is mostly made of glass, which allow for natural ventilation throughout the building. The Solar Heat Gain is 0.8, U Value is 1.27, Visible Light Transmittance is 0.8, and R Value is 0.78. Additionally, there's a free flowing internal space which allows air to ventilate throughout the house. There is also hot water radiant pipes in the floor slab for mechanical heating in the winter when the weather is colder. This heat is being transferred by conduction as it travels through a solid to warm a space. The total Energy Use Intensity is 18 kBTU and the annual carbon emissions is 6000 lb of carbon dioxide. The house is in climate zone nine, meaning the weather is warmer in the summer and cooler in the winter. The climate zone is influenced by the coast and inland.

Our proposed strategies consist of super wall insulation to help warm the house in the winter time when the weather is cooler, clear Aragon triple pane low e windows in insulated fiberglass/vinyl frame which has a better u value as well as visible light transmittance and solar heat gain coefficient in order for cross ventilation to occur successfully as well as helping cool the house in the hotter months and allow ample light during the cooler months. We also extended the overhang so that in the hotter months, there would be more shade and as a result, the air entering the house through cross ventilation would be cooler. The Vertical Shadow Angle would be changed to 63 degrees. Lastly, we added 20 south facing solar panels with a tilt of 34.2 degrees. which would allow for the best efficiency to make the house net zero energy. The total Energy Use Intensity without solar panels is 15 kBTU, and with solar panels is -20 kBTU with the annual carbon emissions being 4500 lb of carbon dioxide without solar panels and -6000 lb of carbon dioxide with solar panels.

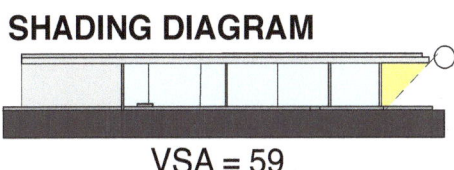

SHADING DIAGRAM

VSA = 59

CASE 22

CASE STUDY 22 - STAHL HOUSE
1635 Woods Dr., Los Angeles CA 90069

CLIMATE ANALYSIS
A

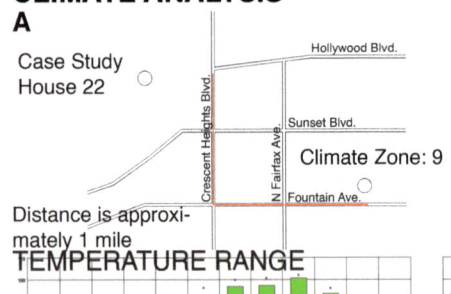
Distance is approximately 1 mile

TEMPERATURE RANGE

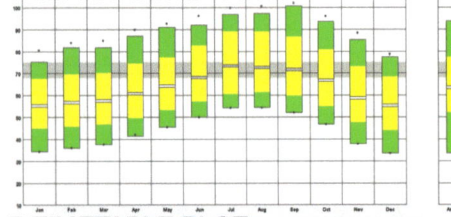

B TIMETABLE PLOT

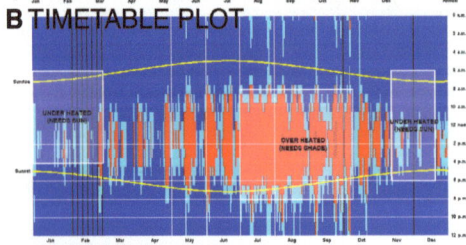

SHADING
C

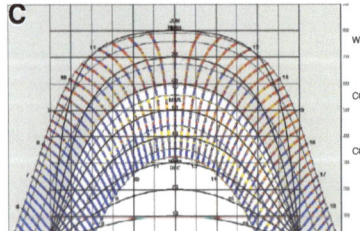

WARM/HOT > 75 F (SHADE NEEDED) 83 HOURS EXPOSED 366 HOURS SHADED
COMFORT > 68 F (SHADE HELPS) 246 HOURS EXPOSED 298 HOURS SHADED
COOL/COLD <68 F (SUN NEEDED) 847 HOURS EXPOSED 672 HOURS SHADED

STRATEGIES
D
1. Comfort
2. Natural Ventilation Cooling
3. Humidification

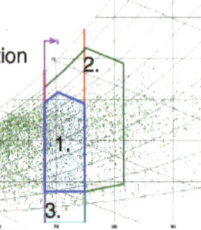

A. Climate Zone: 9 (34N and 118W - Weather Station 59
Temperature Range: Between low 50s to high 70s yearly.
B. Overheated Period:
   May-Nov @8am-8pm
Shade Needed:
   Jul-Sept @8am-8pm
Underheated Period:
   Dec-May and May-Nov @ 8pm-8am
Sun Needed:
   Jan-Feb @6am-6pm
   mid Nov-mid Dec @6am-6pm
E. SHGC: 0.8
   U VALUE: 1.27
   VLT (WINDOWS): 0.8
   R VALUE (WALLS): 0.78

SHADING DIAGRAM

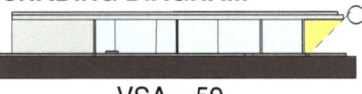

VSA = 59

dotted line= direct sun light
yellow = area where overhang shades the sun

OP= 6ft   HP= 10ft
tan(VSA)= HP/OP
tan(VSA)= 10ft/6ft= 59

There exists an overhang on the south facade with a VSA of 59°.

2030 Examples:

-Heat storage: Thermal mass absorb and store daytime solar heat in winter for release at night

-Glazing: Solar glazing admits direct sunlight into a space for passive heating in winter

-Solar Shading: Overhangs block unwanted sunlight from solar glazing, reducing cooling loads

RECOMMENDED STRATEGIES:
- 8.1% Cooling, add Dehumidification if needed
- 69.3% Heating, add Humidicication
Bioclimatic Strategies:
  -20.8% Sun Shading of Windows
  -7.9% Natural Ventilation Cooling
  -11.8% Passive Solar Direct Gain Low Mass
- Face glass area S to maximize winter sun exposure
- Overhangs/operable sunshades for full shade in summer
- Flat roof in hot dry climate
- Ceiling fans/indoor air motion
- Light colored building materials
- Low mass ventilated 2nd floor
- High mass sun tempered 1st floor
- Long, narrow building floor plan

SUSTAINABILITY DIAGRAM
E

natural light through sun
free flowing internal space
overhang for shading
VSA = 59

cross ventilation through open windows
U Value: 1.27
SHGC: 0.8
VLT: 0.8

hot water radiant pipes in floor slab for natural heating

Annual Carbon Emissions: 6000 lb CO2
EUI: 18 kBTU

CASE 22

IMPROVEMENT IN SHADE
A

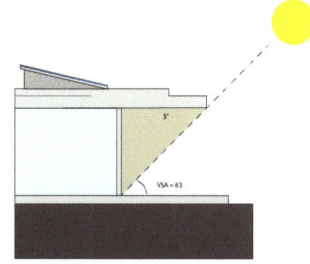

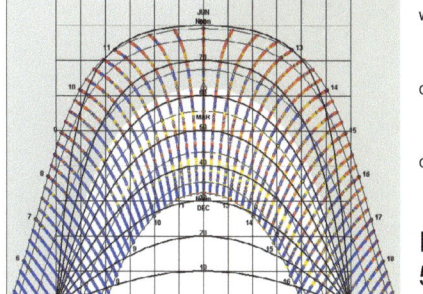

WARM/HOT > 75 F
(SHADE NEEDED)
83 hrs. EXPOSED
366 hrs. SHADED

COMFORT >68 F
(SHADE HELPS)
246 hrs. EXPOSED
298 hrs. SHADED

COOL/COLD <68 F
(SUN NEEDED)
847 hrs. EXPOSED
672hrs. SHADED

Increased VSA from 59 to 63

CLIMATE RESPONSIVE STRATEGIES
B

Proposed Strategies :
1. Solar Panels

2. Clear Argon Tiple Pane Windows for better insulation

3. Wall Insulation for passive water heating
(R value : 1.5)

4. Extended Overhang for improved summer shading
(VLT : 0.1
SHGC: 0.1
U Value: 0.5)

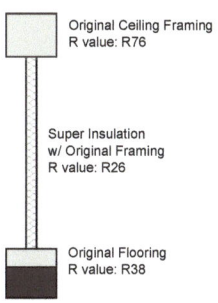

Original Ceiling Framing
R value: R76

Super Insulation
w/ Original Framing
R value: R26

Original Flooring
R value: R38

PERFORMANCE METRICS
C

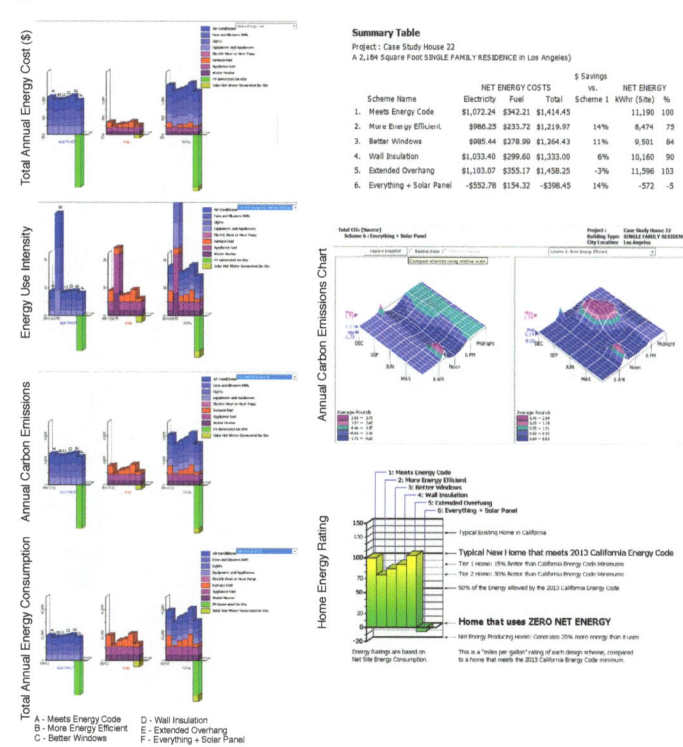

A - Meets Energy Code   D - Wall Insulation
B - More Energy Efficient   E - Extended Overhang
C - Better Windows   F - Everything + Solar Panel

SUSTAINABILITY DIAGRAM
D

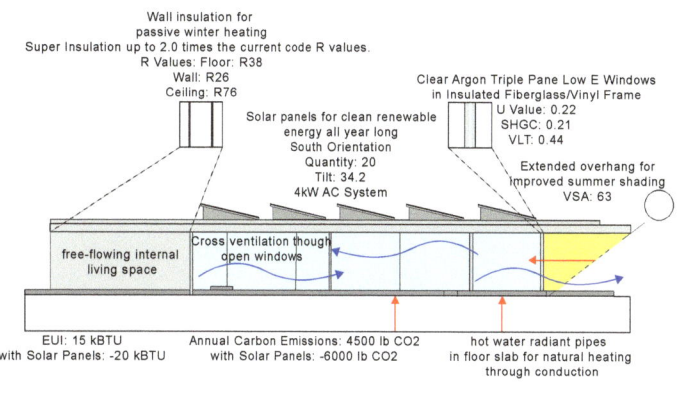

Wall insulation for passive winter heating
Super Insulation up to 2.0 times the current code R values.
R Values: Floor: R38
Wall: R26
Ceiling: R76

Clear Argon Triple Pane Low E Windows in Insulated Fiberglass/Vinyl Frame
U Value: 0.22
SHGC: 0.21
VLT: 0.44

Solar panels for clean renewable energy all year long
South Orientation
Quantity: 20
Tilt: 34.2
4kW AC System

Extended overhang for improved summer shading
VSA: 63

free-flowing internal living space

Cross ventilation though open windows

EUI: 15 kBTU
with Solar Panels: -20 kBTU

Annual Carbon Emissions: 4500 lb CO2
with Solar Panels: -6000 lb CO2

hot water radiant pipes in floor slab for natural heating through conduction

25

Case Study House 22
City, CA | Architect: Pierre Koenig
Group 3: Junhong Wen, Vi Vo, Vivian Liao - Zeng, Apinya Sangrugee, Ying Gao

The Stahl House also known as the case study house 22, was a small lot purchase by Stahl right above Sunset Blvd. Located at California climate zone 9 in Los Angeles, where you experience a typical hot a dry climate. The climate is clearly divided into a cooling period during November to April and a heating period during May to October. The house was an attempt of architectural possibility, however under designed toward remaining the comfort level while staying energy efficient.

The existing issue with the original design includes, thermal mass: limited insulation, and single pane glass. Heating: old furnace consumes more energy and produce less. Shading device: overhang is not suitable for the Vertical Shading Angle, therefore increase the heat gain.

Hereby, we propose a set of solution targeting the energy issue that Stahl House contoured. First, we insulate the exterior walls with R-30 insulations, which improves the current R-value by 1.5 times. Second, we install double pane glass windows, with sliding track, which has a better thermal enclosure, and if need be, cross ventilation can be used. Third, a efficient heating furnace can be install to substitute the old inefficient one. Lastly, a roof PV system can be used to take advantage of the open south facing solar energy, to achieve Net zero energy consumption.

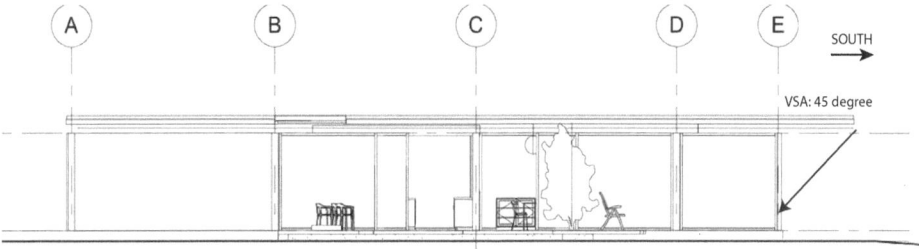

CASE 22

PART I:
Climate and Building Analysis: Stahl House

CLIMATE ANALYSIS

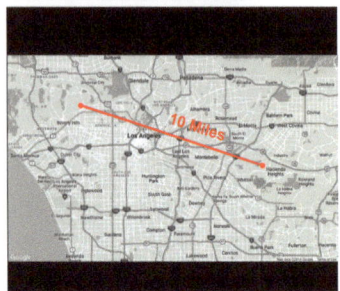 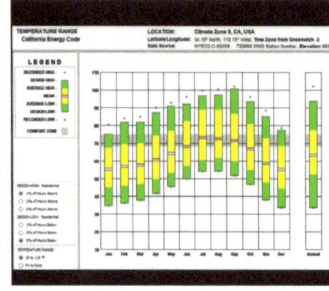 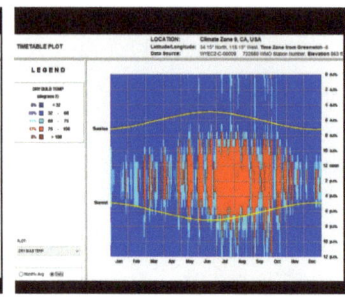 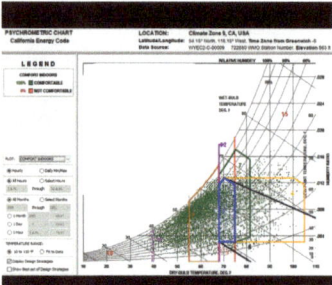

The Stahl house is located within climate zone 9 of California. The house is located 10 miles from the station. Strategies for passive designs can help the house be 80% comfortable throughout the year
Overheated periods started in the middle of the day from May to Nov as shown by the timetable plot. The majority of night times are cool. There are no days or very few days that temperature falls below 32 F or rises above 100 F

EXISTING SHADES

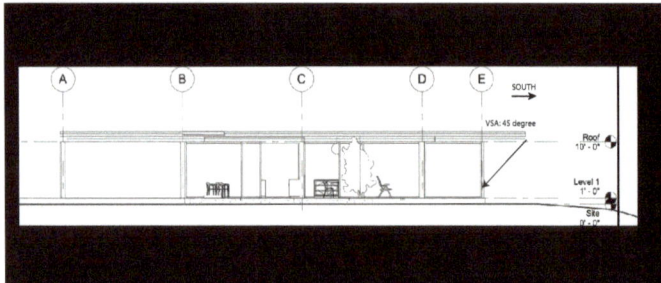 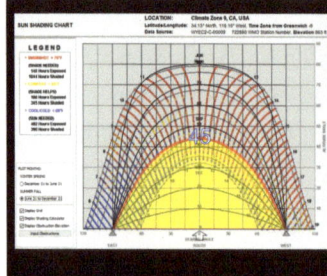 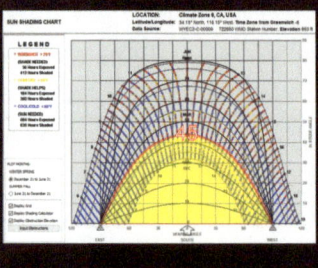

The house employs large overhang to provide shadings. The overhangs have a VSA of 45 degree. According to the sun shading chart, the overhangs provides shade up 90% of the year

BIOCLIMATIC STRATEGIES

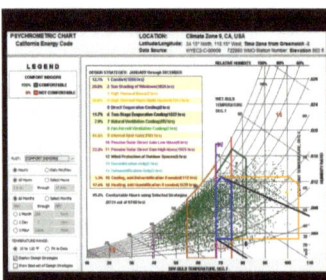

11. Heat gain from lights, people, and equipment greatly reduces heating needs so keep home tight, well insulated (to lower Balance Point temperature)
19. For passive solar heating face most of the glass area south to maximize winter sun exposure, but design overhangs to fully shade in summer
20. Provide double pane high performance glazing (Low-E) on west, north, and east, but clear on south for maximum passive solar gain
24. Use high mass interior surfaces like slab floors, high mass walls, and a stone fireplace to store winter passive heat and summer night 'coolth'
33. Long narrow building floorplan can help maximize cross ventilation in temperate and hot humid climates
35. Good natural ventilation can reduce or eliminate air conditioning in warm weather, if windows are well shaded and oriented to prevailing breezes
37. Window overhangs (designed for this latitude) or operable sunshades (awnings that extend in summer) can reduce or eliminate air conditioning
39. A whole-house fan or natural ventilation can store nighttime 'coolth' in high mass interior surfaces (night flushing), to reduce or eliminate air conditioning
41. The best high mass walls use exterior insulation (like EIFS foam) and expose the mass on the interior or add plaster or direct contact drywall
43. Use light colored building materials and cool roofs (with high emissivity) to minimize conducted heat gain
58. This is one of the more comfortable climates, so shade to prevent overheating, open to breezes in summer, and use passive solar gain in winter
61. Traditional passive homes in hot dry climates used high mass construction with small recessed shaded openings, operable for night ventilation to cool the mass

Shading | Thermal Mass | Flat/Light Color Roof

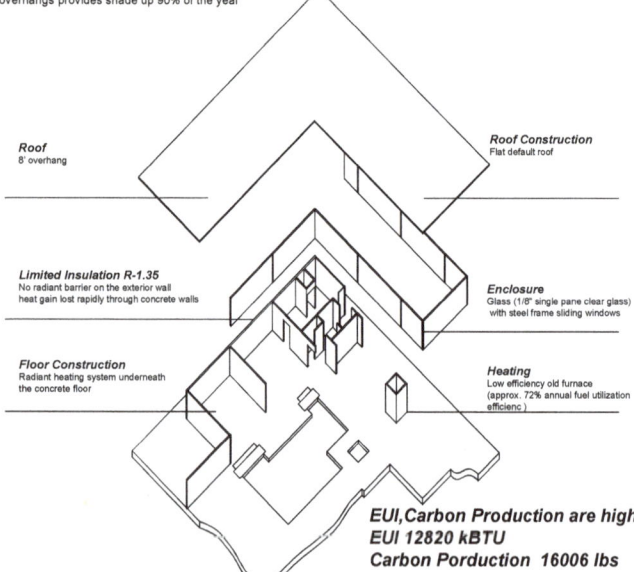

Roof
8' overhang

Roof Construction
Flat default roof

Limited Insulation R-1.35
No radiant barrier on the exterior wall heat gain lost rapidly through concrete walls

Enclosure
Glass (1/8" single pane clear glass) with steel frame sliding windows

Floor Construction
Radiant heating system underneath the concrete floor

Heating
Low efficiency old furnace (approx. 72% annual fuel utilization efficienc)

EUI, Carbon Production are high
EUI 12820 kBTU
Carbon Porduction 16006 lbs

PART II:
Design Proposal: Stahl House

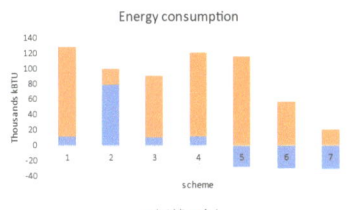

--Scheme 1 is how the Stahl house as built which is a glass wall and concrete structure with overhang.
--Scheme 2 is built with improved furnace with 97 % efficiency.
--Scheme 3 is built with argon filled double pane low-E squared in aluminum frame.
--Scheme 4 is built upgraded insulation to 1.5 current code R-value
--Scheme 5 added 7kW AC system that could make an energy efficient average size home net zero in electrical energy
--Scheme 6 is a combination of scheme 2 to scheme 5
--Scheme 7 is scheme 6 but without the use of heating system, beause according to the climate consultant that heating is not neccesary for most of the time from the existing high thermal masses.

scheme		electricity (kBTU)	fuel kBTU	total kBTU
1	Stahl house as built	12500	115700	128200
2	improved heating cooling	79800	20600	100400
3	improved window	11600	79600	91200
4	improved insulation	12400	108500	120900
5	PV addition	-27700	115700	88000
6	all	-29100	57100	28000
7	all w/o heating	-30300	20600	-9400

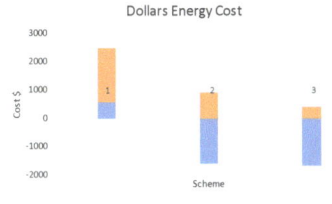

dollars energy cost				
scheme		electricity ($)	fuel $	total $
1	Stahl house as built	590.25	1879.11	2469.36
6	all	-1579.29	928	-651.29
7	all w/o heating	-1662.64	383.49	-1279.15

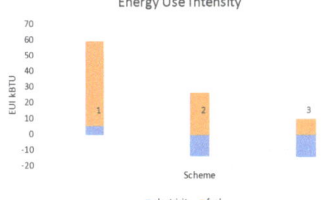

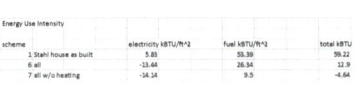

Energy Use Intensity				
scheme		electricity kBTU/ft^2	fuel kBTU/ft^2	total kBTU
1	Stahl house as built	5.83	53.39	59.22
6	all	-13.44	26.34	12.9
7	all w/o heating	-14.14	9.5	-4.64

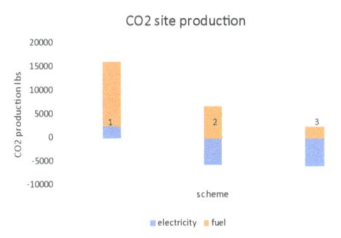

CO_2 site production				
scheme		electricity lbs	fuel lbs	total lbs
1	Stahl house as built	2464.08	13541.92	16006
6	all	-5682.17	6682.38	1000.21
7	all w/o heating	-5978.12	2410.67	-3567.45

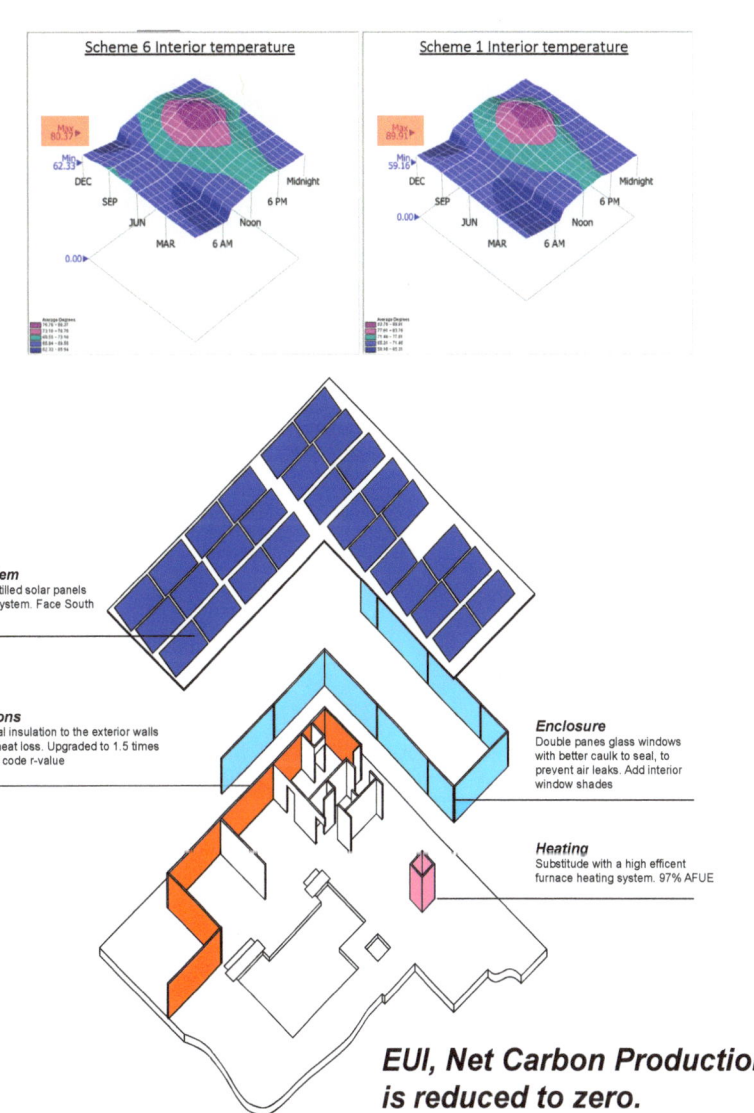

PV System
15 degree tilted solar panels
7 kW AC System. Face South

Insulations
Add thermal insulation to the exterior walls to reduce heat loss. Upgraded to 1.5 times the current code r-value

Enclosure
Double panes glass windows with better caulk to seal, to prevent air leaks. Add interior window shades

Heating
Substitude with a high efficent furnace heating system. 97% AFUE

EUI, Net Carbon Production is reduced to zero.

Case Study House 22
City, CA | Architect: Pierre Koenig
Group 4: Caitlin Mouri, Elizabeth Chan, Melissa Gracia, Michel Williams, Eric Martinez, Jose Martinez

Pierre Koenig's 1960s Stahl House was not designed with energy conservation in mind, and naturally, ideas and technology exist today that were not readily available during the time of construction. The idea of rethinking the design in terms of reducing the house's carbon emissions, is to demonstrate through data analysis how thoughtful design can greatly impact energy conservation. The goal of this project is to take the Stahl house and implement design ideas that will bring the house to a zero-carbon emission status.

The initial phase of the Net Zero Stahl House project began with an assessment of the current atmospheric conditions acting upon the building. The energy expenditure which has the best chance of conservation through passive design systems typically happens during the process of heating and cooling the building, so it was imperative to locate and gather accurate local climate trends in order to determine which systems would be the most effective in bringing the Stahl House to a net-zero status.

This data not only translated a need to warm in the winter and cool during the notoriously hot Summers, but it also gave insight into what hours of the day demanded most attention, as well as the direction of the sun's radiation.

Several design options were considered based on information from a psychrometric chart, but after testing each option's effectiveness, some were dismissed because they required more energy than they could conserve.

Ultimately four primary systems were chosen to be added to the house based on their efficiency: horizontal shading is added to South facing windows to reduce radiant heat, 32 photovoltaic solar panels are placed on the roof to supply the house with clean renewable energy, a water wall is installed to add thermal mass without obstructing the Los Angeles city view, and finally, a green roof is added to provide shading, thermal mass and insulation.

The combination of these systems effectively reduces carbon emissions from the previous estimate of 2,965.17 lbs. per year, to a goal surpassing –2,040.54 lbs. annually. The house now provides more energy than it uses in order to maintain comfortable living conditions for its occupants and can now contribute that surplus energy back to the grid. This project demonstrates that with thoughtful design, houses can become a large part of the solution towards a cleaner environment.

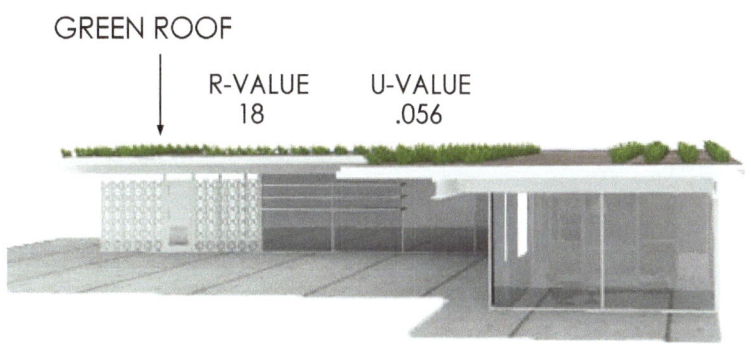

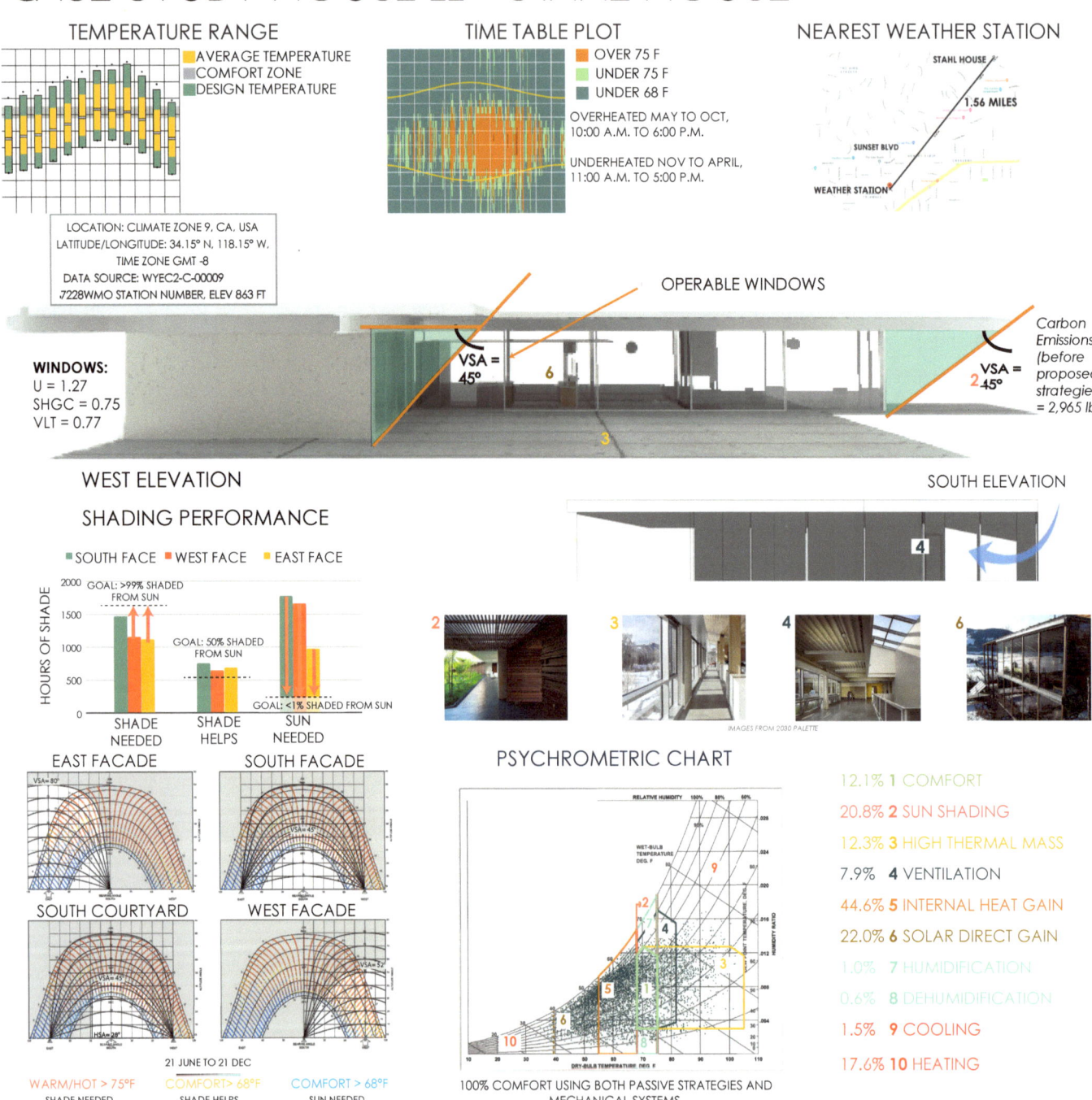

CASE STUDY HOUSE 22 - MODIFICATION PROPOSAL

CASE 22

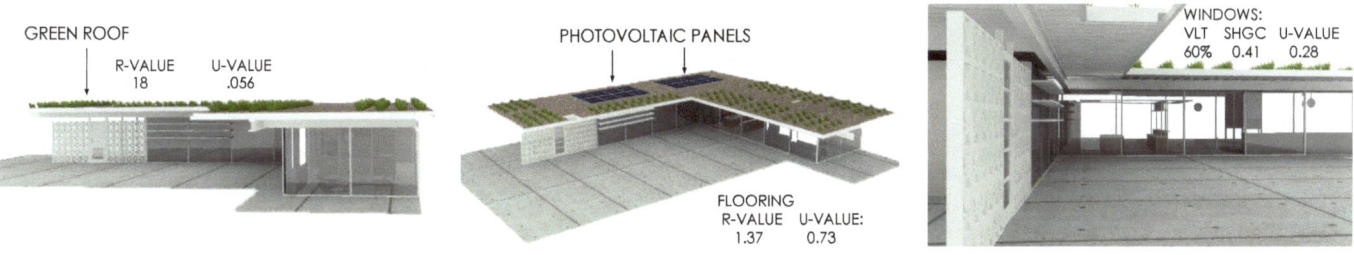

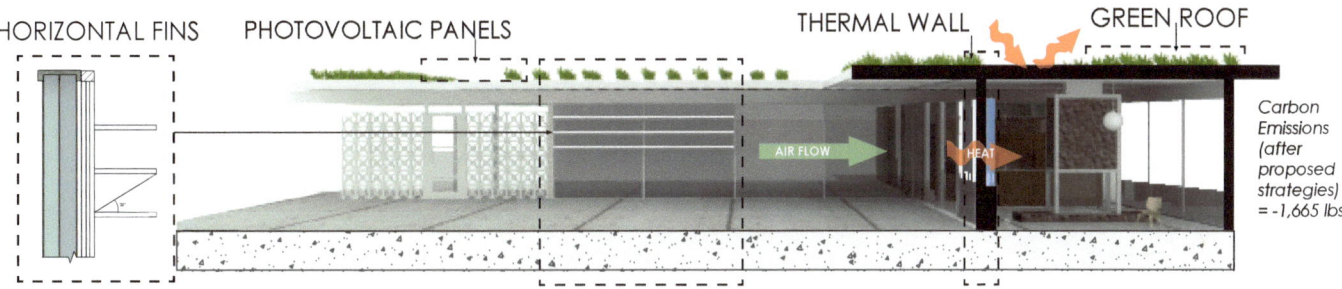

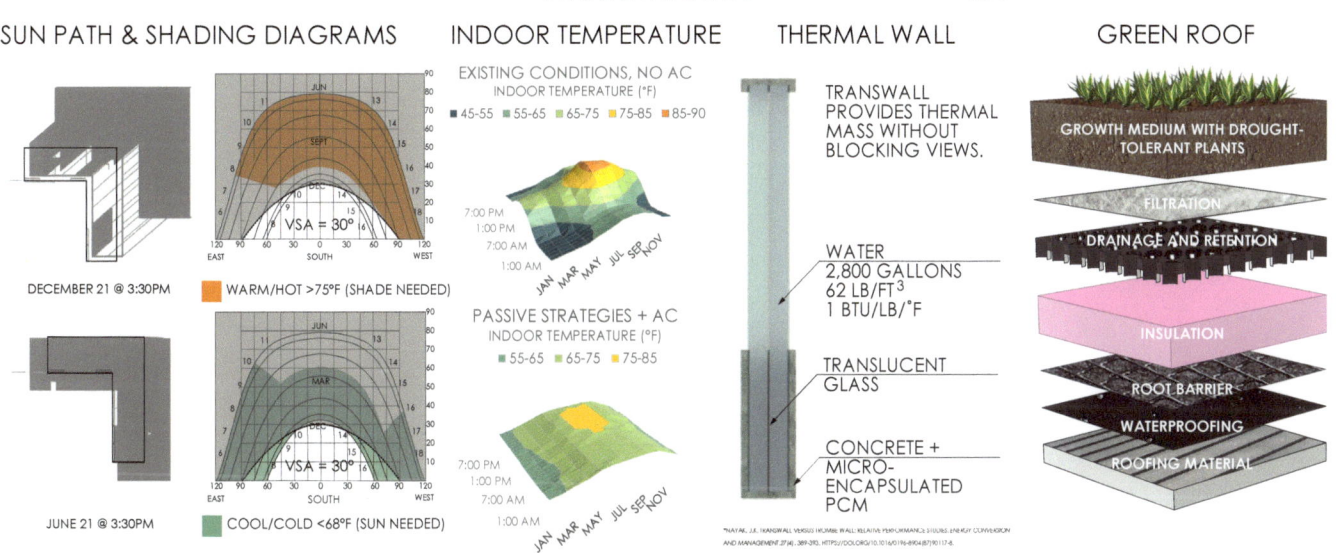

	NET ANNUAL ENERGY COSTS			NET ANNUAL ENERGY (kBtu)			CARBON EMISSIONS (lbs)	EUI (kBtu/ft² yr)
	HEATING[1]	COOLING	TOTAL[2]	HEATING[1]	COOLING	TOTAL[2]		
EXISTING CONDITIONS	$80.98	$27.60	$610.61	3,817.6	634.1	19,389.6	2,965.2	8.6
PASSIVE STRATEGIES + SOLAR*	$0	$0	-$667.88	3,545.3	12,782.2	-5,518.1	-1,664.9	-3.8

1 WATER HEATER
2 INCLUDES LIGHTING AND APPLIANCES
* ALL ENERGY GENERATED ON-SITE

Case Study House 22
City, CA | Architect: Pierre Koenig
Group 5: Ghazi Ghazi, Jose Nunez, Francisco Reyes Sanchez, Isaiah Rojas, Victor Rodriguez

After experimentation with the Stahl House in Heed, through several modifications and iterations our team was able to see the possible contributions it might take to make this house net zero. We started with improving the windows and adding more thermal mass to the east and north side of the building. The windows were upgraded to Clear Argon Triple Pane Loew-E Insulated in Fiberglass/Vinyl frame and the walls were now composed of an Exterior Finish of 4 ½ + SIPS Structural Integrated Panel System 7/16" OSB, 3 5/8" R22 Polystyrene (7/16" OSB). Slight improvements to the floor were made with structural concrete and exposed tile decreasing the U-Value, while upgrading the roof with a PV system angled south toward the sun for maximum efficiency. One of the more interesting additions that drove the project passed net zero was the addition of operable shading that is machine operated and adjust itself to outside weather conditions. The commonality between the modifications between the original standing Stahl House and the proposed net zero version includes the decreasing of the U-Value for many of the upgraded parts, leading to the decrease of the overall amount of BTU/H from approximately 26,602.8 BTU/H to 13,629.06 BTU/H.

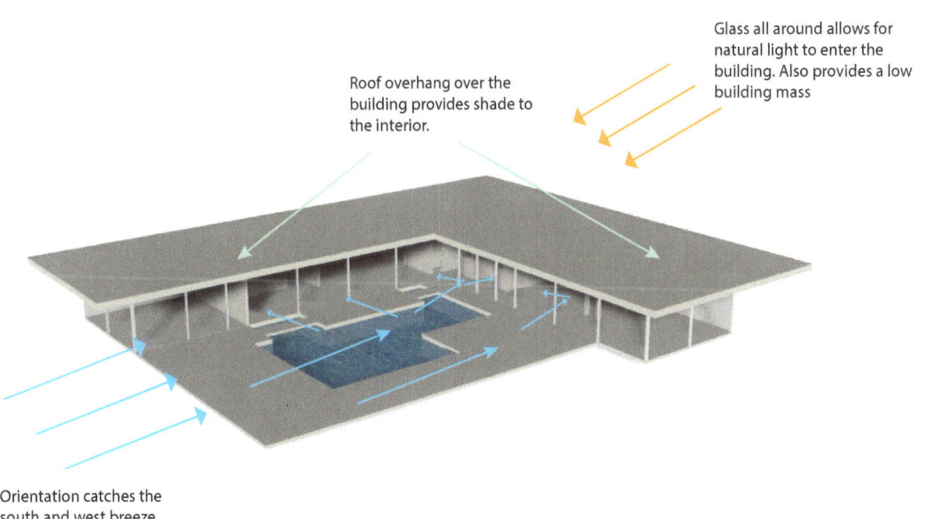

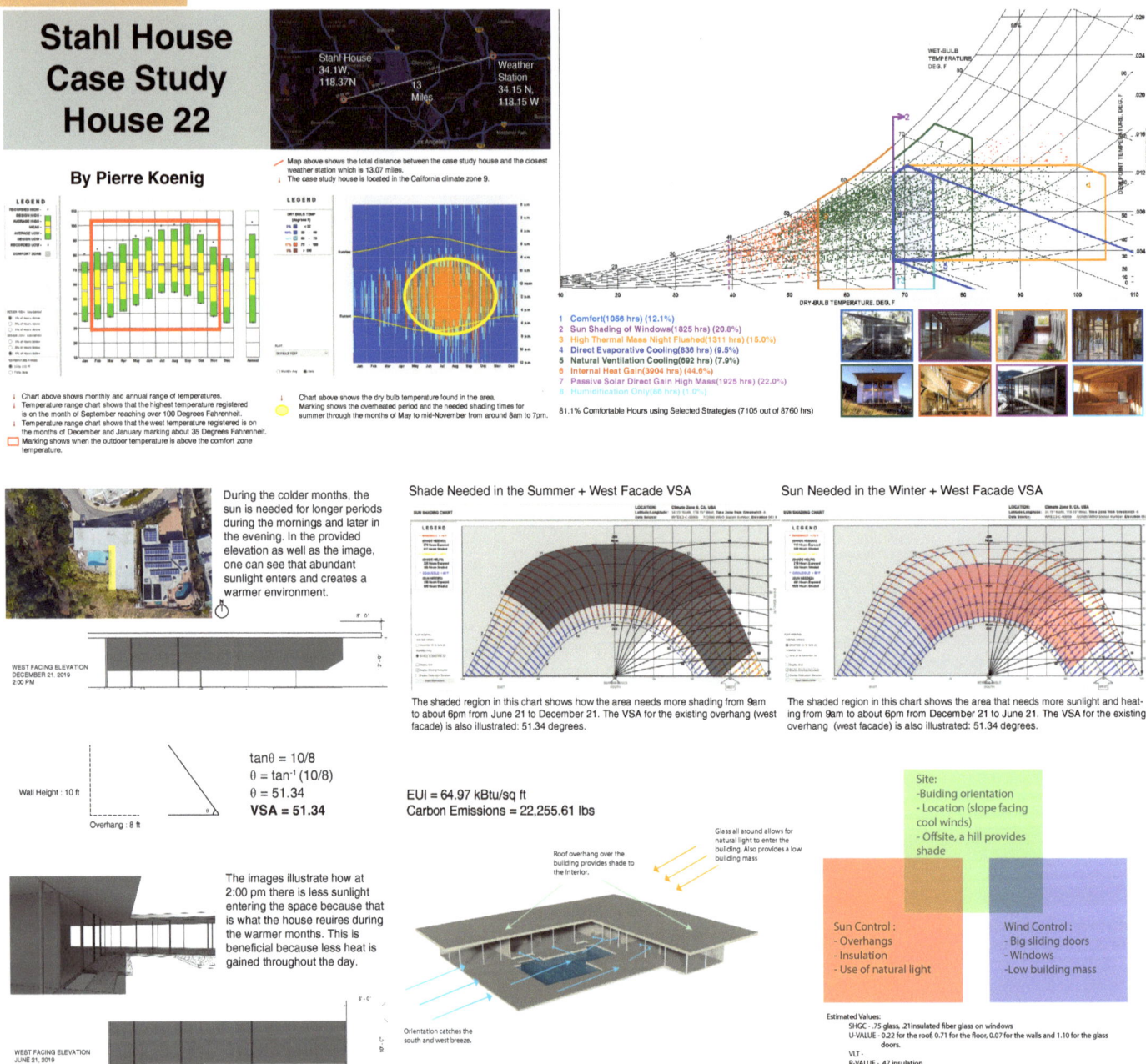

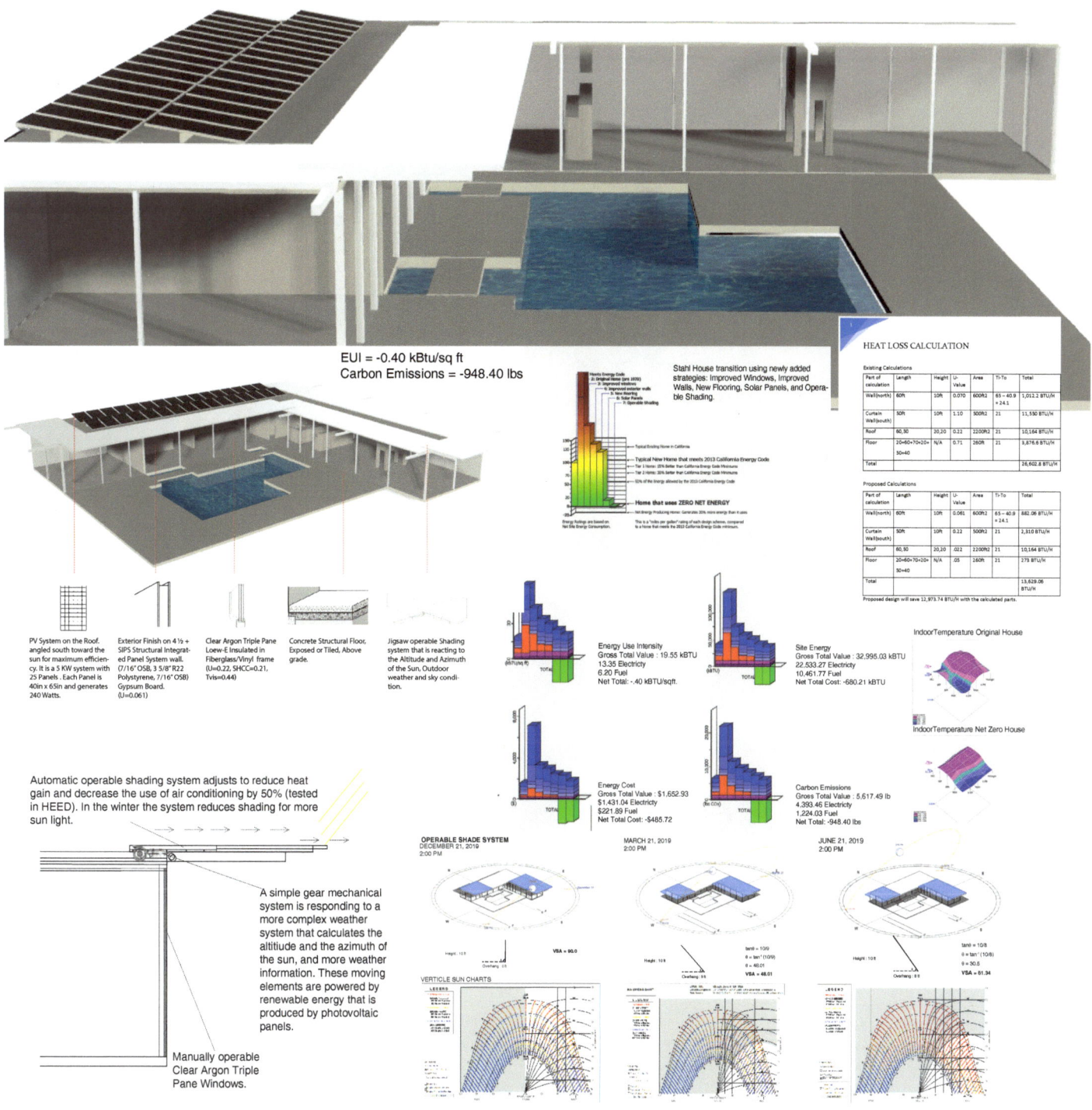

Eames House
City, CA | Architect: Charles and Ray Eames

EAMES

34.029660, -118.519310

Eames House

City, CA | Architect: Charles and Ray Eames
Group 6: Sharifeh Abdallah, Sarineh Nahapedsiraki, Alenoosh Mardroosian, Nerjis G. Kalkan Almonte, Natalie Simba

Eames House is a mid-20th century modern architecture house located in the Pacific Palisades neighborhood of Los Angeles. It was constructed in 1949, by husband and wife design pioneers, Charles and Ray Eames, to serve as their home and studio.

Existing Conditions:
From the temperature range chart, the overall description reads that the main temperature pattern averages at about 47 to 85 degrees through the year. This gives an idea that the climate of the area is coastal and has mild temperatures.

The Timetable chart allows us to see the temperature and because it includes the months in a given year as well as the 24 hours in a day. This information enables us to read what temperature we have every hour of the day. The overheated period in this chart is shaded from the months of June until the end of September from 9:00 am to 4:00pm.

Some of the examples from 2030 palette during summer and winter time. A building form with ample surface area exposed to direct sunlight in winter can easily incorporate passive heating systems. During warm summer months, overhangs block unwanted direct sunlight from solar glazing, reducing cooling loads.

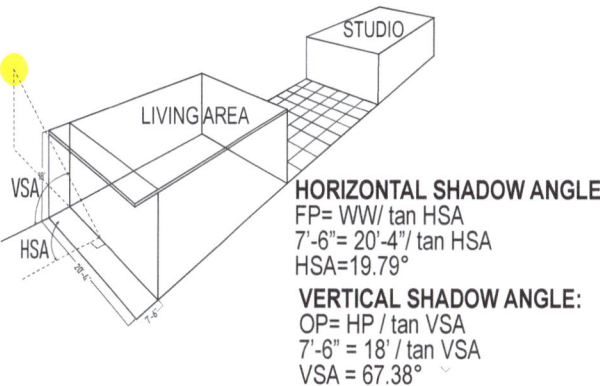

EAMES

NZE PROJECT: EAMES HOUSE

 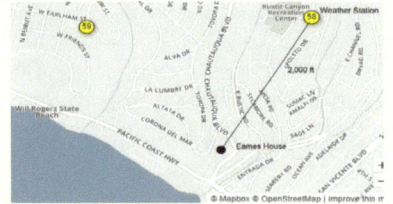 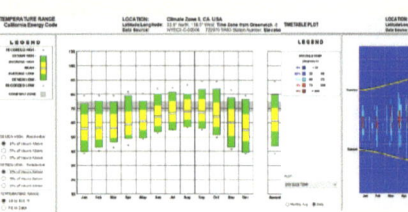 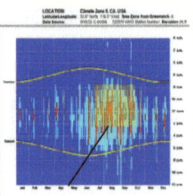

Satellite Map Locating Eames House   Max. and Min Values   Area Need Shading

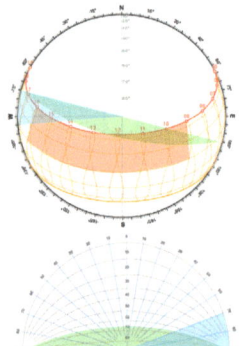 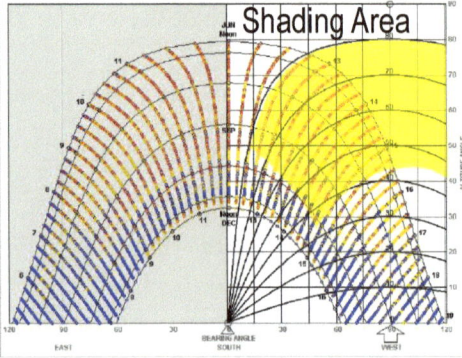 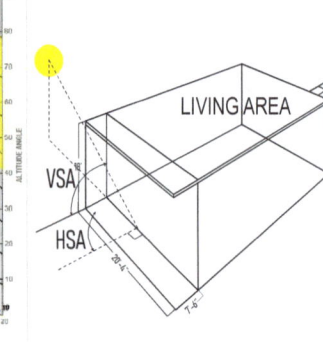

HORIZONTAL SHADOW ANGLE:
FP= WW/ tan HSA
7'-6" = 20'-4"/ tan HSA
HSA = 19.79°

VERTICAL SHADOW ANGLE:
OP= HP/ tan VSA
7'-6" = 18' / tan VSA
VSA = 67.38°

PSYCHROMETRIC CHART
LOCATION: Climate Zone 6, CA, USA
Latitude/Longitude: 33.9° North, 118.5° West Time Zone from Greenwich -8
Data Source: WYEC2-C-00006 722970 WMO Station Number, Elevation 98 ft

98.8% Comfortable Hours by Using the Flowing Strategies:
1. Comfort (14.4%)
2. Natural Ventilation Cooling (6.3%)
3. Internal Heat Gain (58.6%)
4. Heating, Add Humidification if Needed (21.5%)

- Cemesto Cladding Colored Panels
- Standard Steel window with glass
- Steel roof deck
- Concrete retaining wall
- Interior Walls - Gypsum Board
- Floor

Existing EUI Value of the House = 63.10 KBTU/sq.ft

NET Total CO_2 Produced = 21,780.04 lbs

Exterior R Values:
Cemesto Panels (0.25" thick): 0.06
Single Pane Windows (0.25" Thick): 1.04
Steel: N/A
Concrete Masonary 12": 1.28
Total R Values: 2.38
Total U Value: 0.42
Visible Transmitance for Single Pane Windows: 89% of daylight
Approx. (SHGC): 0.81
Approx. SHGC for all Windows: 7.29

Existing Climate Responsive Strategies:
Natural Lighting and Ventilation
Natural Sun Shading System
Overhang for Shading

Examples From 2030 Palette:

Form for Heating in Winter.   Solar Shading in Summer

EAMES

Based on existing over-heated period:
For vertical shadow angle of 35°
Horizontal shading element needed:
OP= HP / tan VSA
OP= 18' / tan (35°)
OP= 25.7'

For horizontal shadow angle of 70°
Vertical shading element needed:
FP= HP / tan VSA
FP= 20'-4" / tan (70°)
FP= 7.39'

New Proposal:
For Vertical Shadow Angle of 55°
Horizontal shading element:
OP= HP / tan VSA
OP= 18' / tan (55°)
OP= 12.6'
Exiting vertical shading
FP= WW/ tan HSA
FP= 20'-4"/ tan (70°)
FP= 7.4'

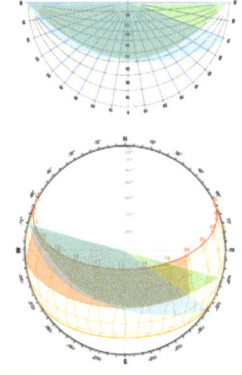
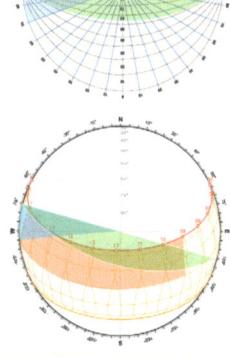

Walls
Walls changed from 2x4 Wood Studs with no cavity and gypsum board interior to 4.5" sips structural Integrated panel system. It changed U value from 0.356 to 0.061

Windows
The exciting clear single pane 1/8" glass in aluminum frame windows replaced with clear argon triple pane low-e insulated fiberglass windows. This replacement will reduce BTU from 1.27 to 0.22 and SHGC from 0.75 to 0.21

Insulation
The house had no insulation, it built in 1949. Adding insulation to house It upgraded to 1.5 times current code R-values

Infiltration
Infiltration changed from very poorly sealed to passive house standard (tm) extrem tight Air Sealing requirement. Specific Leakage Area went down from 6.0 to 0.3. Air Changes at

Energy Use Intensity Before and After Applying the Strategies.

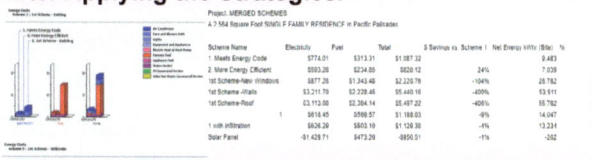

SUMMARY TABLE: The metric table shows a comparison of the design statistics before and after these strategies. The existing building loses 406% in Net Energy costs whereas our proposed NZE Design saves 24% in Energy Code.

New EUI Value is -0.35 KBTU/sq.ft
New NET Total CO₂ Produced is -2,464.97 lbs

INSULATION Upgraded to house 1.5 times current code R-values

WINDOWS Argon triple pane low-e insulated fiber glass windows

WALLS 4.5" sips structural Integrated panel system

Infiltration between walls and ceiling
Infiltration between walls and windows

Description of Proposed Sustainable Strategies in House

Performane Metrics

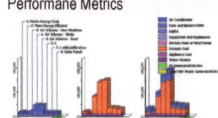
Energy Costs-Dollar energy

Energy Costs-Site Energy kWH/Sqft

Energy Costs-site energy kbtu is 12,426.55 kWh (131% of Design1),
3,855.04 Electricity
8,607.51 Fuel
12,725.43 Minus PV Site Energy Saved
NET TOTAL SITE ENERGY is -262.88 kWh

GROSS TOTAL VALUE is $1,094.55 (101% of Design1)
$621.35 Electricity
$473.20 Fuel
$2,051.06 Minus PV Generated on Site
NET TOTAL COST is $-956.51(-88% of Design1)

GROSS TOTAL VALUE is 16.58 kBtu/sq.ft (128% of Design1)
5.13 Electricity
11.45 Fuel
16.93 Minus PV Site Energy Saved
NET TOTAL COST is -0.35 kBtu/sq.ft (ZNSE=-3% of Design 1)

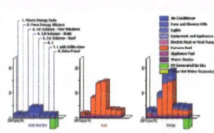
Energy Costs-Site EUI kWH/Sqft

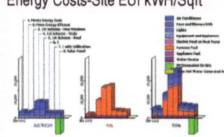
Energy Costs-Coc site production lbs

GROSS TOTAL SITE ENERGY is 12,462.55 kWh (131% of Design1)
3,855.04 Electricity
8,607.51 Fuel
12,725.43 Minus PV Site Energy Saved
NET TOTAL SITE ENERGY is -262.88 kWh (ZNSE=-3% of Design 1)

GROSS TOTAL CO₂ Equivalent is 6,000.75 (121% of Design1)
2,564.60 Electricity CO₂ Equivalent
3,436.15 Fuel CO₂ Equivalent
8,465.72 Minus PV Generated on Site CO₂ Equivalent
NET TOTAL SITE ENERGY is -2,464.97 lbs
(ZNSE=50% of Design 1)

HOME ENERGY RATING: The chart above describes the different strategies incorporated to arrive to having a Net Zero Energy building. The targeted areas to enforce this efficiency include walls, installing new windows, infiltration, solar panels and roof.

Eames House
City, CA | Architect: Charles and Ray Eames
Group 7: Maribel Ruiz, Yeganeh Malouhi, Nauryzbek Naurbekov, Natalie Valle, Kristin Lorentzen

The Eames House sits withing the region of Climate Zone 6. The nearest weather station to the beach side residence is the Santa Monica Municipal Airport which is only 4.08 miles away. The climate in this area is temperate throughout most of the year. The original design of the Eames House have single glaze windows with little to no insulation. The average low temperature is 57.1 °F. The average high is 70.5 °F. The main issue with the Eames House is the amount of energy consumed from using the heater during the cold months.

The psychometric chart displays the daily climate, temperature, and humidity throughout the year in relation to a person's comfort zone. Most of the days that are underheated and out of the comfort zone which occur during the cold months of the year. The other days that are outside of the comfort zone are during the warm months due to overheating but this does not nearly occur as often as underheating. The design strategies that are suggested by climate consultant and incorporated into our design are high thermal mass, direct evaporative cooling, and natural ventilation cooling in the warm months. Internal heat gain and passive solar design are incorporated in the cold months. With these strategies alone, there is already 84.4 % of comfort throughout the year. The other 15.6% is solved through the design proposals to improve performance and achieving net zero energy.

Recommended Strategies from the 2030 palette (concepts & case studies): Since our main issue is heating during the winter, these two concepts allow us to maintain internal heat while keeping alterations to the house at a minimum. In the 44th Street House, heat storage is incorporated in the residence. Concept: Thermal mass – masonry floors, walls and/or ceilings – absorb and store daytime solar heat in winter for release at night. A large portion of the sunlight (heat gain) admitted into a space during the daytime must be stored inside the same space for release during the nighttime hours. In the Vieider House, direct gain is incorporated through double-pane glazing. Concept: Solar glazing – this admits direct sunlight into a space for passive heating in winter. Solar glazing (facing the equator) is sized to admit enough sunlight on an average sunny winter day to heat a space over the full 24-hour period.

The Eames House is primarily constructed of prefabricated steel pieces, windows and an 8" thick CMU wall on the South East portions of the building. It has had problems with air leakage and rust on the steel and a new wall assembly in the portions of the wall without windows. Our proposal is to upgrade the solid wall to 2x6 at 24" on center with advanced framing techniques to maximize insulation. The exterior wall will also include a brick facade which will help with additional thermal mass.

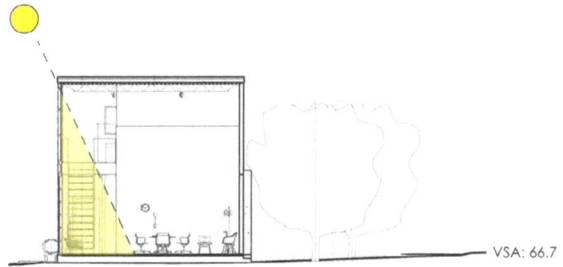

VSA: 66.7

EAMES HOUSE | NET ZERO ENERGY DESIGN PROPOSAL

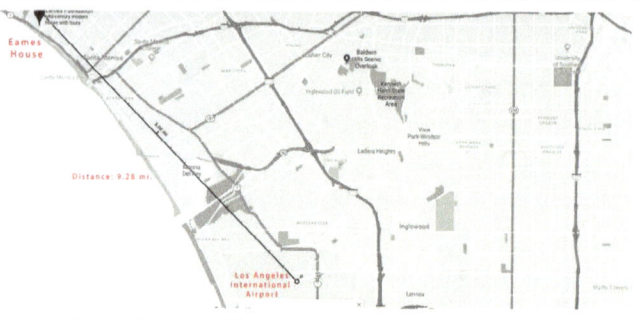

The Eames House sits within the region of Climate Zone 6. The nearest weather station to the beach side residence is Los Angeles International Airport.

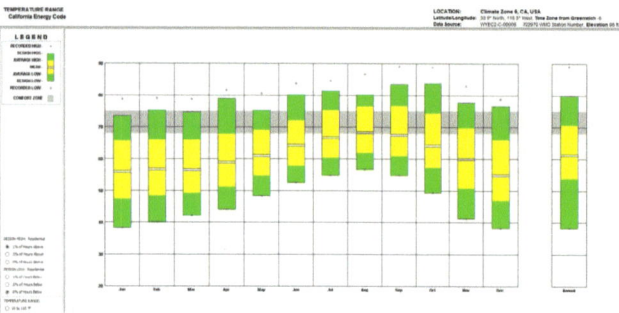

Temperature Range

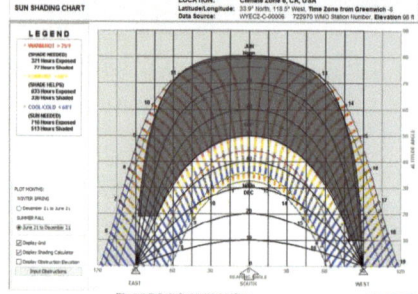

Overheated Time Table Plot for June 21 - December 21

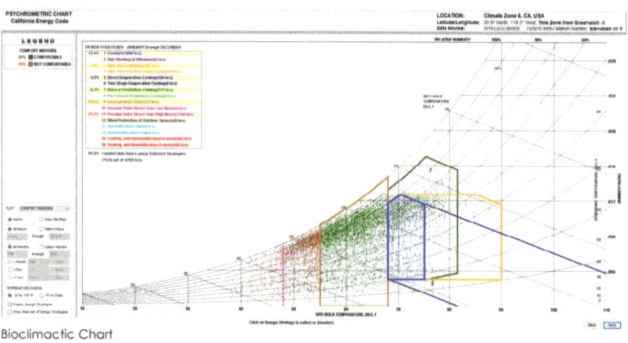

Bioclimactic Chart

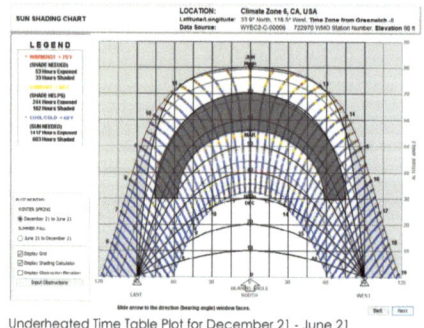

Underheated Time Table Plot for December 21 - June 21

Case Study:
Structure: 44th Street House
Architect: Joseph Hurley Architects
Location: 44th Street, Seattle, Washington, USA

Case Study:
Structure: VisibJer House
Architect: Egger-Atchner-Seidl
Location: Valdaora de Sopra, Bolzano, Italy

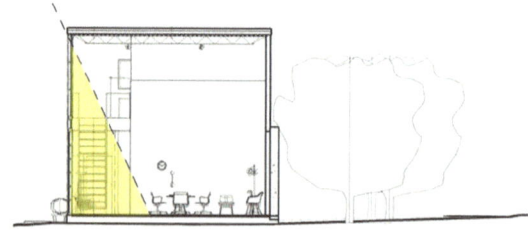

VSA: 66.7

Project By Kristin Lorentzen, Natali Valle, Maribel Ruiz, Yeganeh Malouhi, Nauryzbek Naurbekov

EAMES

EAMES HOUSE | NET ZERO ENERGY DESIGN PROPOSAL

EXTERNAL SHADING SYSTEM
Our proposal features exterior slatted blinds that are automated hourly to reduce internal heat gain during summer months and to increase internal heat gain in the winter months.

HEATING AND COOLING
A mini-split or heat pump in each of the buildings would provide a simple solution for both heating and cooling while also being highly energy efficient.

WALL ASSEMBLY

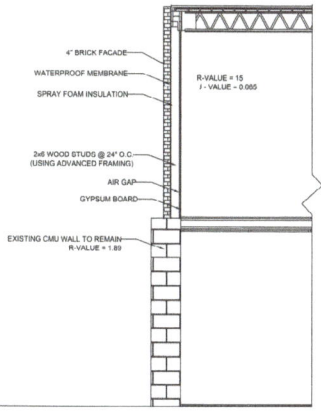

- 4" BRICK FACADE
- WATERPROOF MEMBRANE
- SPRAY FOAM INSULATION
- 2x6 WOOD STUDS @ 24" O.C. (USING ADVANCED FRAMING)
- AIR GAP
- GYPSUM BOARD
- EXISTING CMU WALL TO REMAIN R-VALUE = 1.89

R-VALUE = 15
U-VALUE = 0.065

Material	Width	Calc R value
Brick	4"	0.80
Closed Cell Spray Foam	5"	32.5
Inside Air Layer	1/2"	0.68
Gypsum Board	1/2"	0.45

R1+R2+R3+R4 = 34.43

CARBON REDUCTION
A tree can absorb as much as 48 pounds of carbon dioxide per year. This proposal will not only negate its own carbon footprint, but it will actually reduce carbon by around ~837 lbs/year. This means the new proposal is roughly the equivalent of planting almost 18 trees per year, every year.

SOLAR ENERGY
A 5kW system of this size is about 25 solar panels, which takes up roughly 400 sq/ft of roof.

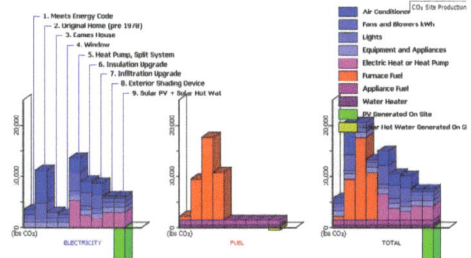

Solar Hot Water Heater
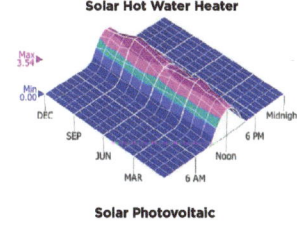

Solar Photovoltaic
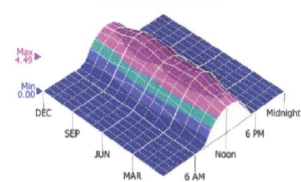

Original Home Building Performance	
Total annual energy consumption (kBtu)	47,240 kWh/year
Total annual energy cost in dollars	$3,030.00
Energy Use Intensity EUI	50.62 kBtu/sq ft
Annual Carbon Emissions (Net Total)	10,896 lbs or 7.36 lbs/sqft

Energy Reduction by Category	
Clear Double Pane Low-E Squared in Insulated Vinyl Frame (U=0.30 SHGC = 0.46 Tvis=0.58)	
Total annual energy consumption (kBtu)	29,808 kWh/year
Total annual energy cost in dollars	$1,977.12
Energy Use Intensity EUI	37.61 kBtu/sq ft
Annual Carbon Emissions (Net Total)	10,530 lbs or 4.74 lbs/sqft
	Energy Reduction = 36.9%
	Cost Reduction = 34.7%
	Carbon Reduction = 47%
Best Available Heat Pump, Split System (Cooling SEER=20.0, HSPF = 9.5)	
Total annual energy consumption (kBtu)	33,929 kWh/year
Total annual energy cost in dollars	$9,247.00
Energy Use Intensity EUI	42.81 kBtu/sq ft
Annual Carbon Emissions (Net Total)	21,754 lbs or 8.05 lbs/sqft
	Energy Reduction = 28.2%
	Cost Increase = 205%
	Carbon Increase = 9.4%
Insulation at 1.5 times Current Code R-Value + New Wall Assembly	
Total annual energy consumption (kBtu)	36,847 kWh/year
Total annual energy cost in dollars	$2,401.00
Energy Use Intensity EUI	46.49 kBtu/sq ft
Annual Carbon Emissions (Net Total)	2,496 lbs or 0.92 lbs/sqft
	Energy Reduction = 22%
	Cost Reduction = 21%
	Carbon Reduction = 87.5%
Infiltration Upgrade: Passive House Standard (0.3 SLA, 0.6 ACH50)	
Total annual energy consumption (kBtu)	43,667 kWh/year
Total annual energy cost in dollars	$2,817.00
Energy Use Intensity EUI	55.10 kBtu/sq ft
Annual Carbon Emissions (Net Total)	18,440 lbs or 6.82 lbs/sqft
	Energy Reduction = 7.6%
	Cost Increase = 0.1%
	Carbon Reduction = 7.3%
Exterior Shading Device - Automated Exterior Blinds	
Total annual energy consumption (kBtu)	64,570 kWh/year
Total annual energy cost in dollars	$4,071.00
Energy Use Intensity EUI	81.48 kBtu/sq ft
Annual Carbon Emissions (Net Total)	26,955 lbs or 9.97 lbs/sqft
	Energy Increase = 36%
	Cost Increase = 34%
	Carbon Reduction = 35%
Solar Photovoltaics + Solar Hot Water Heater	
Total annual energy consumption (kBtu)	34,429 kWh/year
Total annual energy cost in dollars	$2,098.00
Energy Use Intensity EUI	43.00 kBtu/sq ft
Annual Carbon Emissions (Net Total)	11979 lbs or 4.43 lbs/sqft
	Energy Reduction = 27%
	Cost Decrease = 30%
	Carbon Reduction = 40%

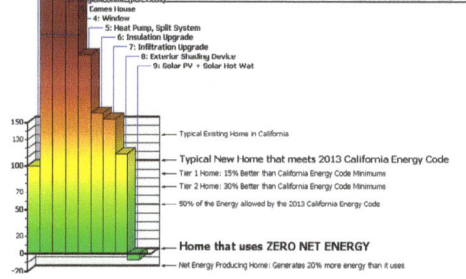

LOW E-GLASS
Low E-Glass is the single most important element in this design proposal. Replacing all windows with clear double pane low-e glass will reduce energy consumption by almost 40 percent. It also contributes to cutting the carbon emissions by almost 50 percent.

49

Eames House
City, CA | Architect: Charles and Ray Eames
Group 8: Frank Ruedas, Dung Quoc Dinh, Rita Jirjees, Kimberly Carlisle, Noah Lemus

The Eames house is located on a cool but moderate climate just off the coast in the Pacific Palisades. The use of deciduous trees around the building allows for sun shading in the summer and passive solar heating in the winter. The buildings footprint is long and narrow to allow for cross ventilation from the moderate winds from the ocean and evening cooling from the eastern desert winds. The slender plan of the building also allows for a longer south facing surface area to capture more solar heat during the daytime.

We had to make some changes in order to make the Eames house a net zero house. To do this, we changed the glazing, added a cool roof, fan forced ventilation, solar panels, water heating system, and electric furnace. The original house had clear, single pane glass in an aluminum frame. We updated the glazing to be a tinted, triple pane reflective glass which will decrease solar gain during the summer months. This new glazing ultimately effects the U value. The trees in front of the house block some solar heat gain already, however, the improvement in glazing still adds a benefit to the overall efficiency of the building. The second change that we made is the cool roof. With an already flat roof, the addition of a cool roof will reduce energy costs and improve occupant comfort. Thirdly, adding a whole house fan increases ventilation throughout the house, improving occupant comfort. Adding an 8 kW AC 40 panel solar system and the solar water heating system we provide the house with a system that can rely on solar energy for electricity demands and hot water. The solar panels face south west with a 30 degree tilt in order to maximize the energy from the sun. In addition, replacing the low-efficient furnace with an electric furnace allows for heating costs to be offset by the solar panel energy that will be generated. While the house is not one hundred percent net zero energy, we have significantly reduced energy consumption and increased occupant comfort with the addition of the previously stated strategies.

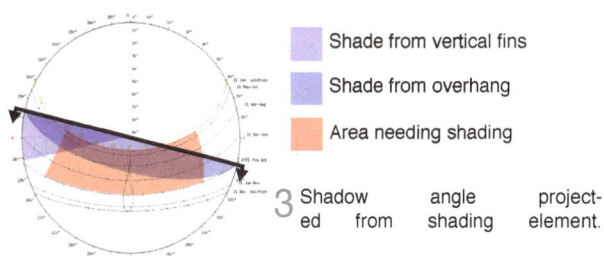

3 Shadow angle projected from shading element.

EAMES

EAMES HOUSE
CASE STUDY HOUSE NO. 8

CLIMATE and BUILDING ANALYSIS

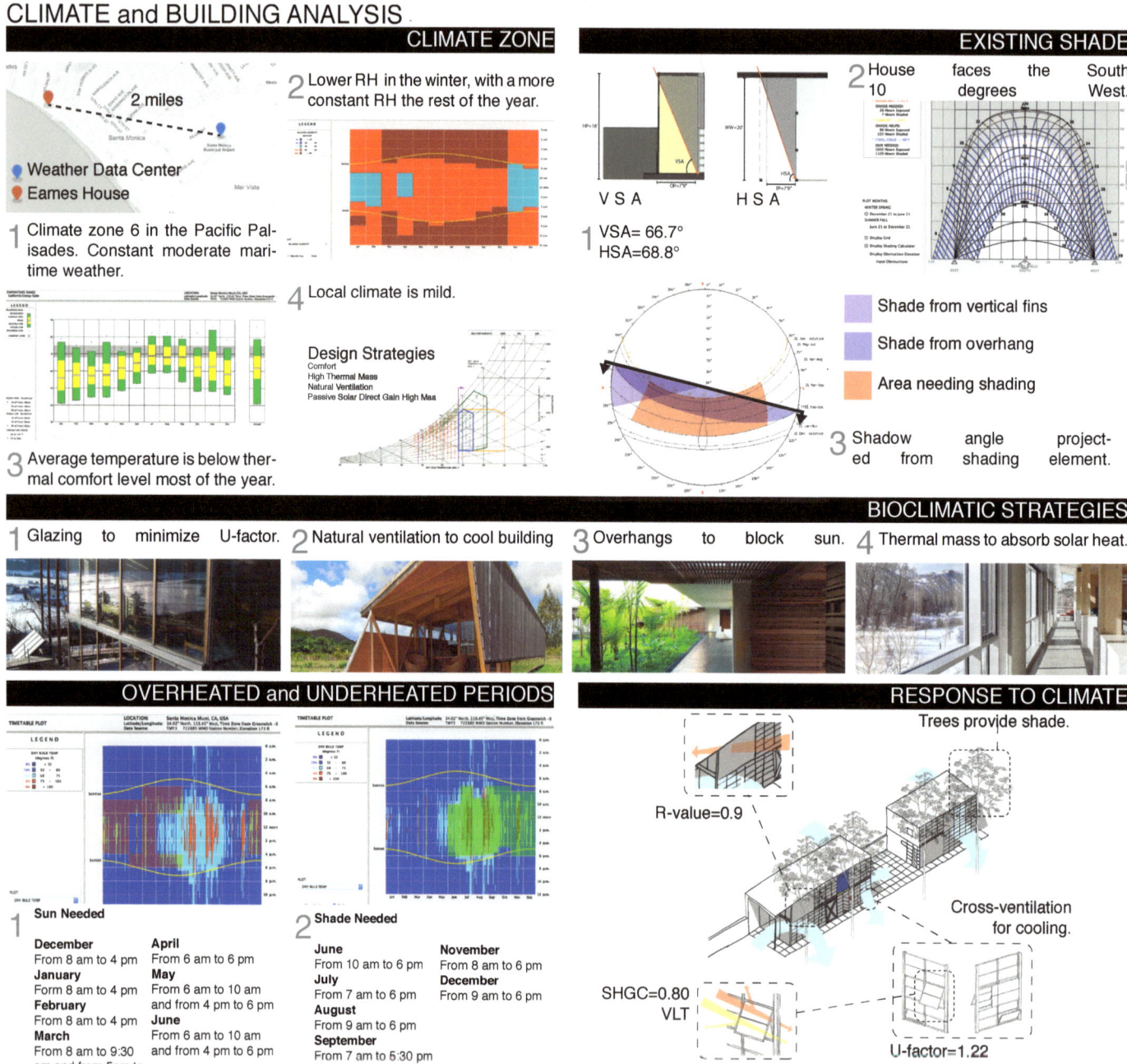

CLIMATE ZONE

1. Climate zone 6 in the Pacific Palisades. Constant moderate maritime weather.
2. Lower RH in the winter, with a more constant RH the rest of the year.
3. Average temperature is below thermal comfort level most of the year.
4. Local climate is mild.

Design Strategies
- Comfort
- High Thermal Mass
- Natural Ventilation
- Passive Solar Direct Gain High Mass

1. VSA= 66.7°
   HSA= 68.8°

EXISTING SHADE

2. House faces the South 10 degrees West.
3. Shadow angle projected from shading element.

- Shade from vertical fins
- Shade from overhang
- Area needing shading

BIOCLIMATIC STRATEGIES

1. Glazing to minimize U-factor.
2. Natural ventilation to cool building
3. Overhangs to block sun.
4. Thermal mass to absorb solar heat.

OVERHEATED and UNDERHEATED PERIODS

1. Sun Needed
   - **December** From 8 am to 4 pm
   - **January** Form 8 am to 4 pm
   - **February** From 8 am to 4 pm
   - **March** From 8 am to 9:30 am and from 5pm to 6pm
   - **April** From 6 am to 6 pm
   - **May** From 6 am to 10 am and from 4 pm to 6 pm
   - **June** From 6 am to 10 am and from 4 pm to 6 pm

2. Shade Needed
   - **June** From 10 am to 6 pm
   - **July** From 7 am to 6 pm
   - **August** From 9 am to 6 pm
   - **September** From 7 am to 5:30 pm
   - **October** From 9 am to 4:30 pm
   - **November** From 8 am to 6 pm
   - **December** From 9 am to 6 pm

RESPONSE TO CLIMATE

Trees provide shade.
R-value=0.9
Cross-ventilation for cooling.
SHGC=0.80 VLT
U-factor=1.22

EUI (before)=55.31 kBTU/sq.ft — Carbon Emissions=22,959.48 lbs

EAMES HOUSE
CASE STUDY HOUSE NO.8

DESIGN PROPOSAL

IMPROVED SHADE SYSTEM

Changing VSA from 67 degrees to 55 degrees increases 25% more shaded time during heated period and still leaves enough solar energy access to the building during winter time.

VSA=55°
Because
OP=HP/tan(VSA)
Therefore
OP=18'/tan(55)=12.6'

HP=18'
VSA = 55 degree
OP= 12' 7"

CLIMATE RESPONSIVE STRATEGIES

tinted triple pane reflective glazing

Heat Gain — U-value = 0.15
— SHGC=0.26
Light — VLT=0.45

Tinted Triple Pane Reflective Glass

SUSTAINABLE CONCEPT DIAGRAM

- Solar Domestic Hot Water
- 8 kw AC System 60 Panels
- Cool Roof
- Tinted Triple Pane Reflective Glass
- Building Wrap High Standard
- Deciduous trees for shade

EUI (after)=-18. kBTU/sq.ft - Carbon Emissions=-12,574.43 lbs

PERFORMACE METRICS

ANNUAL COOLING AND HEATING ENERGY (kBTU)

Total Annual / Cooling / Heating
(kBTU)

ANNUAL COOLING AND HEATING $

Total Annual / Cooling / Heating
($)

EUI
(kBTU/sq.ft.)

CARBON EMISSIONS
(lbs)

Original — NZE

AVERAGE DEGREES YEARLY TEMPERATURE

Deciding to omit the use of an AC unit in the NZE design of the Eames House, the yearly temperature is still comfortable as shown in plot.

- 71.46-74.63
- 68.30-71.46
- 65.13-68.30
- 61.96-65.13
- 58.79-61.96

Max 74.63
Min 58.79

Eames House
City, CA | Architect: Charles and Ray Eames
Group 9: Kristal Audish, Upavee Amarasinghe, Jared Pablo, Krissandra Perez, Daniela Pomalaza

The Eames house is located in a suburban neighborhood on the bluffs in the Pacific Palisades. The house was built for Ray and Charles Eames, one building to serve as their home and the other to function as a studio. It was built in an attempt to create affordable but innovative housing for post-war Americans. The house is located in climate zone 6, because of its proximity to the ocean the Eames house experiences a cool climate and natural ventilation. The house is also surrounded by trees which help to shade the house and block strong winds.

The buildings are on a North, North-East to South, South-West axis with the back of the building facing West. The Eames House responds to the climate by using sustainable design strategies such as horizontal overhangs. The use of external shading is much more effective than internal shading. The overhangs protect the building from sunlight on the south facing façade, but these overhangs would allow some winter sun to come through and heat the space. When used effectively, external shading methods can eliminate approximately ninety percent of solar radiation. It is important that the Eames House uses these shading mechanisms efficiently because it is located in a warm and moist climate.

The sustainability strategy we are proposing is an operable wall/ sliding glass wall on the east facade of the building. Operable walls provide many sustainability benefits in both the open and closed position. When they are closed they can reduce glare and control UV and air leakage, as well as condensation. The energy efficient frames and glazing of the wall also improves general building performance. Operable walls, when opened, allow for improved daylighting, increased views, and easy access to the outdoors and fresh air. They also allow you to have additional usable area without increasing the building's footprint. We also increased the overhangs which shades windows from excess sun and overheating and can also protect the building from rain damage. We also opted to add solar panels because of the energy savings they provide. These strategies reduced the carbon to -2296.29 and the energy to 2858.66 kWh.

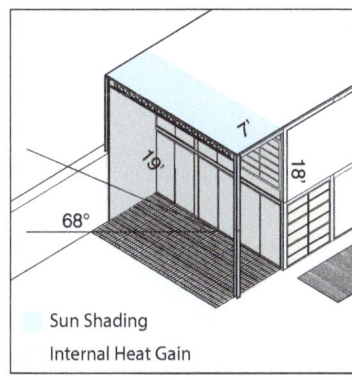

EAMES HOUSE
Pacific Palisades CA

Timetable Plot
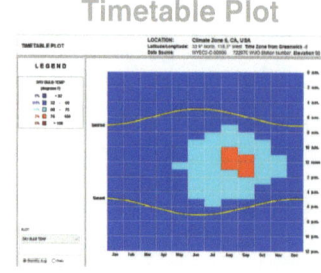

Psychometric Chart
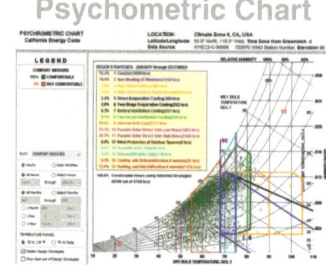

Temperature Range
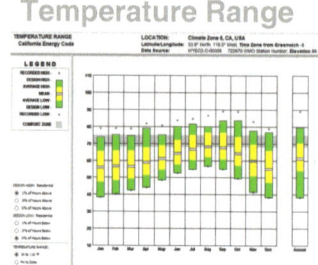

The Eames House is in Climate Zone according to Climate Consultant. The reference city for zone 6 is Los Angeles (LAX). This zone is in Southern California consisting of beaches and the inland area. The weather in this region is considered mild. Summers are often cooled by ocean winds. When the humidity is high, the temperature tends to be low remaining at a comfortable level. This climate zone receives an abundance of solar radiation which is beneficial to the use of solar heating. According the temperature range, the recorded high barely climbing up t0 90°F, and the coldest at 38°F. The average and design highs typically fall within the comfort zone, confirming that climate zone 6 is very mild and a comfortable environment to reside in.

Overheated and Underheated Period

Climate Zone 6

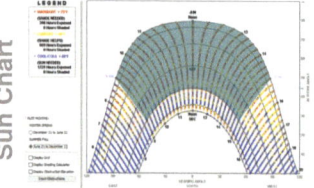

The time periods when shade is recommended is during the months of June to October from 9 AM - 3 PM.

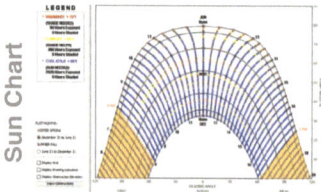

The underheated periods are in the months of December to March from 5 PM to 8 AM, when it is typically under 66°F.

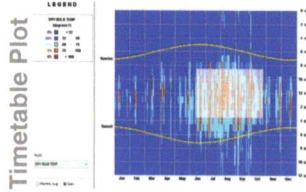

Shade is vital from around 9 AM - 3PM in the months of June to October.

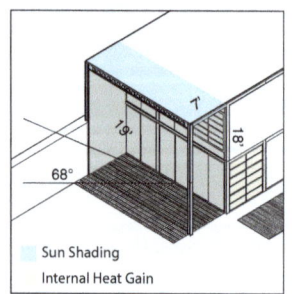

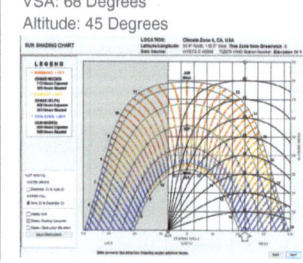

Horizontal Overhang
VSA: 68 Degrees
Altitude: 45 Degrees

Suggested Bioclimaic Strategies:
- solar shading
- direct gain: glazing
- direct gain: heat storage

Examples from 2030 Palette
Solar Shading   Direct Gain Glazing   Direct Gain Heat Storage

Disadvantages:
Overheating and over exposure due to large windows spanning the majority of facade

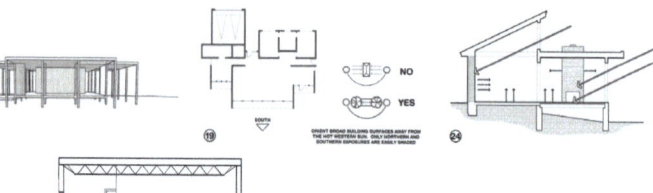

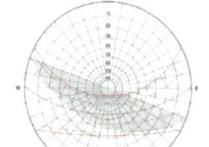

Vertical Sun Path Diagram

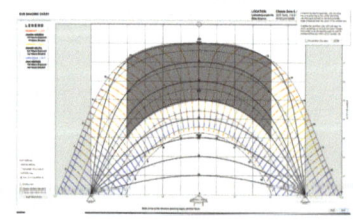

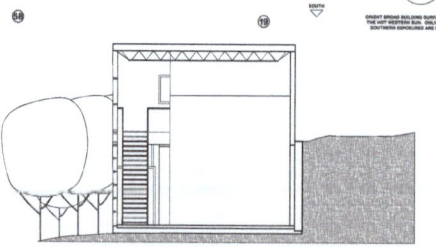

EAMES HOUSE
Pacific Palisades CA

Improving Existing Climate Strategies
Proposed Climate Strategies

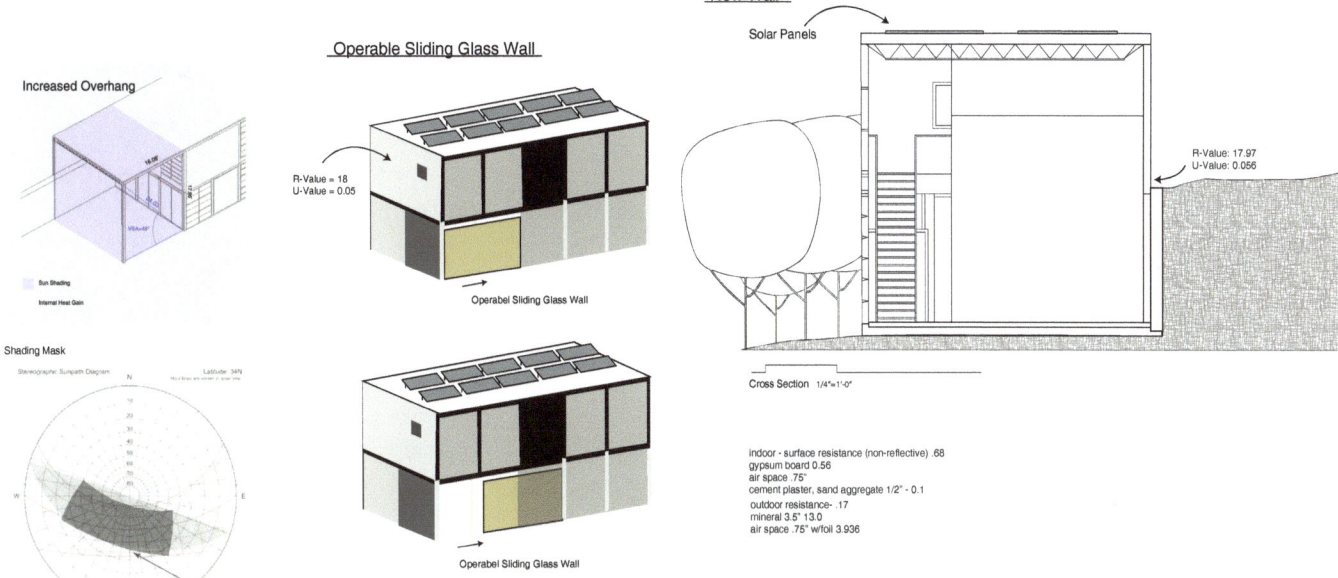

indoor - surface resistance (non-reflective) .68
gypsum board 0.56
air space .75"
cement plaster, sand aggregate 1/2" - 0.1
outdoor resistance- .17
mineral 3.5" 13.0
air space .75" w/foil 3.936

HEED analysis of the home

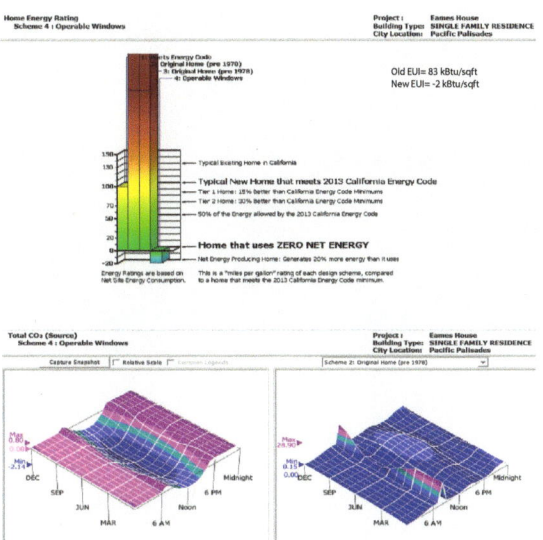

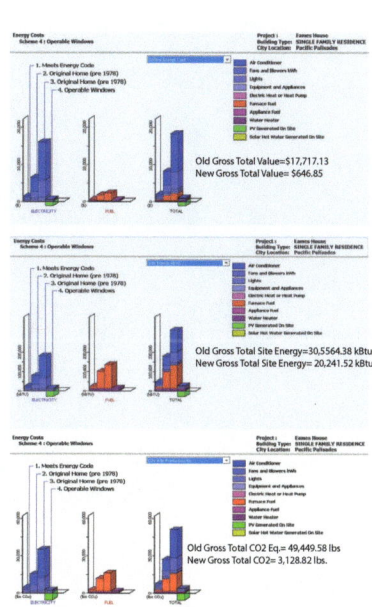

Eames House
City, CA | Architect: Charles and Ray Eames
Group 10: Joshua Ryan, Olivia Nilges, Heather Gallacher, Alex Gonzalez, Emane Henderson

The Eames house is a modern home that has a narrow floorplan and is made up of a concrete foundation, glass, wood, and stucco walls, an asphalt roof, and steel frame. The home is placed in the Pacific Palisades (Latitude/Longitude 34.0300 N, 118.51194 W). The weather is generally warm throughout the year, and experiences more wind currents. With the information gathered, and the help of climate consultant, we found the Eames house was located climate in zone 6. The Eames House is not known for net zero energy. The large concrete wall spanning across the east, and the windows spanning across the west make it hard for the house to benefit from cross ventilation. The windows in the current home do not prevent sunlight, and uv rays from the interior, making the home exposed to sunlight and the objects inside to deteriorate. On the southern side of the home there is an overhang in place, but it does not block the majority of sunlight throughout the year.

In order for our group to get the home to zero net energy we needed to take the existing problems and use strategies and resources in order to find ways to fix the problems. The strategies we are implementing into the home are updated windows, insulation, a larger overhang, solar panels, and infiltration. The current condition of the windows is a clear single 1.8" glass in aluminum framing; this will be updated to a triple-glazed clear glass with a wood or vinyl with a u-value of .34. The existing walls are being changed from continuous insulation to super insulation, 2x current code. The overhang will be updated by making it longer so that the sun is blocked for longer amounts of time, as for the infiltration, it will be updated to extremely tight air sealing, specific leakage area: 0.3. Lastly, we want to add 20 solar panels to the roofing of the home for a better source of energy.

The strategies we are implementing into the home for a zero net energy are updated windows, insulation, a larger overhang, solar panels, and infiltration. The current condition of the windows is a clear single 1.8" glass in aluminum framing; this will be updated to a triple-glazed clear glass with a wood or vinyl with a u-value of .34. The existing walls are being changed from continuous insulation to super insulation, 2x current code. The overhang will be updated by making it longer so that the sun is blocked for longer amounts of time, as for the infiltration, it will be updated to extremely tight air sealing, specific leakage area: 0.3. Lastly, we want to add 20 solar panels to the roofing of the home for a better source of energy.

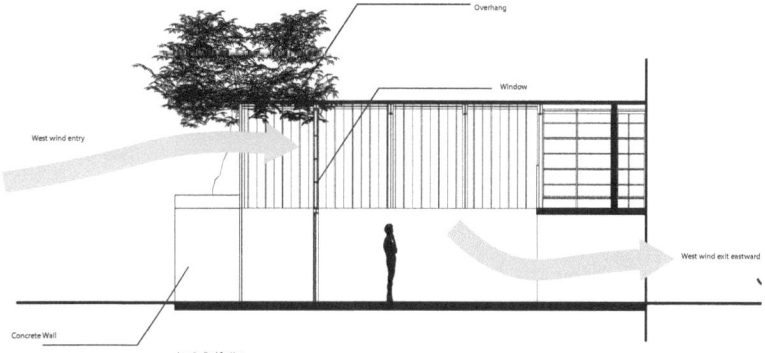

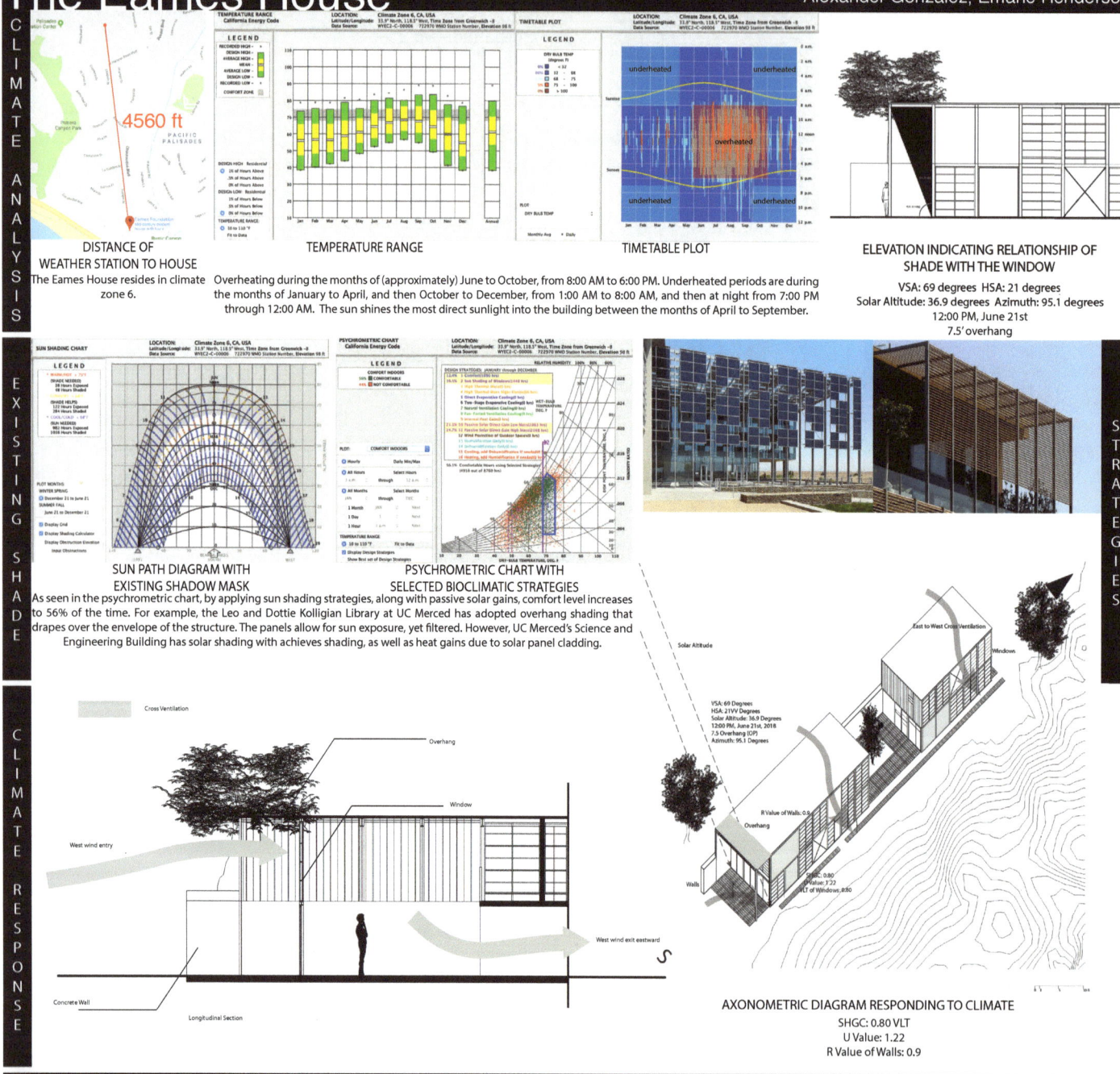

EAMES

Heather Gallacher, Olivia Nilges, Joshua Ryan, Alexander Gonzalez, Emane Henderson

PROPOSED SHADE

Overall Overhang: = 15'-0"
Added Overhang: = 7.5'

OLD	NEW
VSA: 69.0	VSA:53.1 degrees
HSA: 31.0	HSA: 33.7 degrees

The strategies we are implementing into the home for a zero net energy are updated windows, insulation, a larger overhang, solar panels, and infiltration. The current condition of the windows is a clear single 1.8" glass in aluminum framing; this will be updated to a triple-glazed clear glass with a wood or vinyl with a u-value of .34. The existing walls are being changed from continuous insulation to super insulation, 2x current code. The overhang will be updated by making it longer so that the sun is blocked for longer amounts of time, as for the infiltration, it will be updated to extremely tight air sealing, specific leakage area: 0.3. Lastly, we want to add 20 solar panels to the roofing of the home for a better source of energy.

PERFORMANCE METRICS

NET ENERGY COSTS

ELECTRICITY	FUEL	TOTAL	SAVINGS PER SCHEME ($)	NET ENERGY
$515.55	$276.27	$791.81	0%	100
$399.42	$239.14	$638.56	19%	81
$3408.02	$344.94	$3753.97	-374%	252
$602.74	$263.83	$338.91	-51%	10

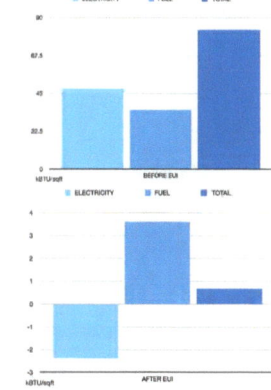

Existing House vs. House after Proposed Changes

Material	R Value (Before)	R Value (After)	Percentage	Total (Before)	Total (After)
Outside Air Film	0.17	0.17			
Stucco	0.08	0.08			
Plywood	0.62	0.62			
Insulation	0	30			
Gypsum Board	0.56	0.56			
Inside Air Film	0.68	0.68			
Total	2.11	32.11			
U Value	0.473	0.031	75%	(0.473)(0.75) = 0.355	(0.031)(0.75) = 0.023
Outside Air Film	0.17	0.17			
Stucco	0.08	0.08			
Plywood	0.62	0.62			
3.5 Wood	4.38	4.38			
Gypsum Board	0.56	0.56			
Inside Air Film	0.68	0.68			
Total	6.49	6.49			
U Value	0.154	0.154	25%	(0.154)(0.25) = 0.038	(0.154)(0.25) = 0.038

SUSTAINABLE CONCEPT

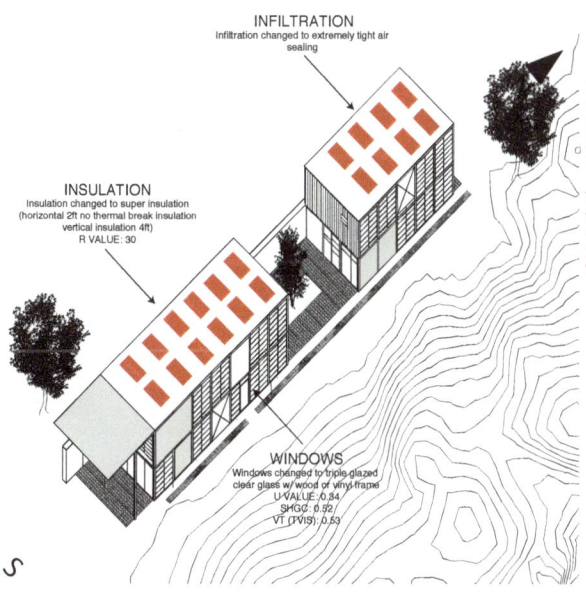

INFILTRATION – Infiltration changed to extremely tight air sealing

INSULATION – Insulation changed to super insulation (horizontal 2ft no thermal break insulation vertical insulation 4ft) R VALUE: 30

WINDOWS – Windows changed to triple-glazed clear glass w/ wood or vinyl frame
U-VALUE: 0.34
SHGC: 0.52
VT (TVIS): 0.53

Single-Pane Windows 1/8" glass w/ aluminum framing
U-Value=0.89
SHGC=0.64
TVIS=0.86

Triple-glazed clear glass with a wood or vinyl
u-value= 0.34
SHGC= 0.52
VT (TVIS)= 0.53

Concrete

CLIMATE RESPONSE

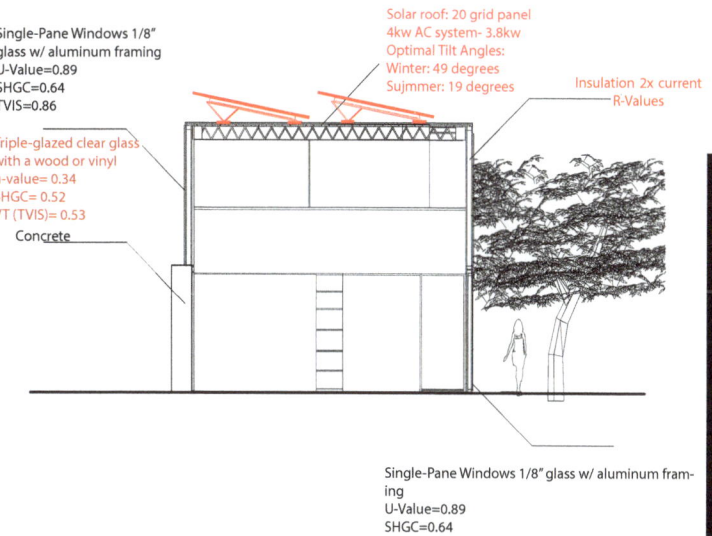

— Proposed strategies

Solar roof: 20 grid panel
4kw AC system- 3.8kw
Optimal Tilt Angles:
Winter: 49 degrees
Sujmmer: 19 degrees

Insulation 2x current R-Values

Single-Pane Windows 1/8" glass w/ aluminum framing
U-Value=0.89
SHGC=0.64
TVIS=0.86

Kappe House
City, CA | Architect: Ray Kappe

KAPPE

34.041451, -118.515678

Kappe House
City, CA | Architect: Ray Kappe
Group 11 : Noah Mora, Trevor Kubo, Michael Joya, Vincent Nguyen

Climate zone 6 is typically known to have warm and dry summers, morning fogs and clear winters. Ray Kappe's house is located in a hilly neighborhood with deep deciduous trees. Virtually most of the house is made of glass and as a result large amounts of light enters into the space. However, this did create an ambient atmosphere inside the house. Although the trees do assist in limiting the amount of heat and light that enters into the building, it is not enough. Another concern of the house is the amount of heat that is retained. There is no features existing to maintain heat levels in the house during the winter months. The main concerns with this house is the capture of heat in winter and how the house will stay ventilated while also bringing in sufficient natural lighting.

There are multiple proposals that will enhance the house. First, we looked at the insulation of the home so that heat can be retained and excess heat can be deterred. This step implemented an exterior finish on 8" concrete block and interior insulation with gypsum board. Since a majority of the house is made of wood, we thought a change in materiality to concrete would offer better heat retaining features inside the with a focus in the flooring. Also, the upgrade from single pane glass windows to triple pane vinyl frames were implemented to the design so that light and heat is filtered into the house smoothly. These ideas develop into passive strategies that limits the amount of fuel and electricity that is used. To further regulate and assist the lighting and heating in the house, the addition of a large fan and improved furnace were added for when uncomfortables levels are reached in the home.

Finally, in order to reach net zero energy standing from the home, a solar energy system was introduced so that the home can produce its own energy and be self sufficient. Thirty solar panels with six kW of energy along with three panels intended to be a solar water heating system were placed on the roof facing south to maximize the amount of energy being absorbed. The final product of the house is a net zero energy structure that is able to be self sufficient. The energy levels being exuded by the home is countered with multiple passive strategies.

Scheme	Annual Energy Cost	Savings Compared to Scheme 3	
Meeting Energy Code	$2213.54	$1559.86	59%
More Energy Efficient	$1341.63	$2431.77	35%
Iteration 1	$3662.20	$111.20	97%
Iteration 2	$2317.22	$1456.18	61%
Iteration 3	$2167.60	$1605.80	57%
Iteration 4	$2505.16	$1268.24	66%
Iteration 5	$3584.84	$188.56	95%
Iteration 6	$1368.79	$2404.61	36%

FAN AND FURNACE

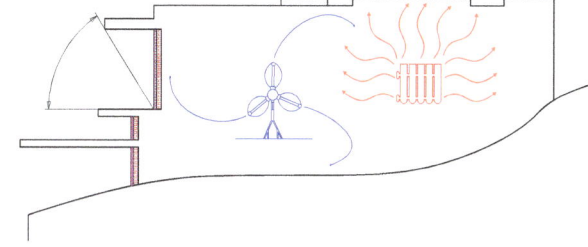

KAPPE

KAPPE RESIDENCE CLIMATE ANALYSIS

PSYCHROMETRIC CHART

EFFECTIVE DESIGN STRATEGIES
1. Internal Heat Gain
2. Passive Solar Direct Gain High Mass
3. Sun Shading of Windows
4. Natural Ventilation Cooling
5. Direct Evaporative Cooling

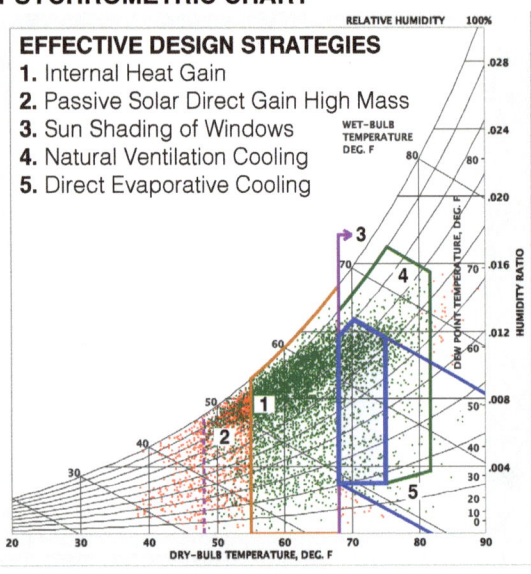

CLIMATE ZONE 6

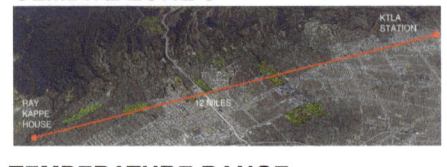

TEMPERATURE RANGE

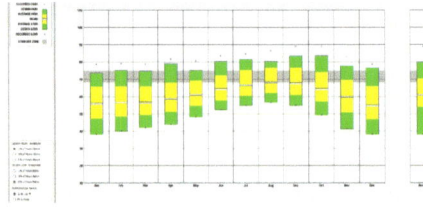

TIME TABLE

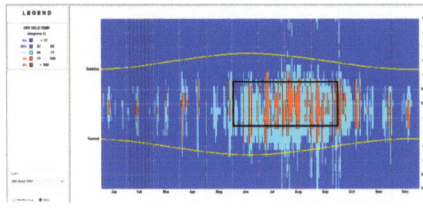

SUN SHADING

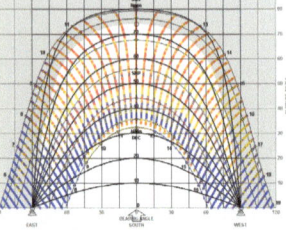

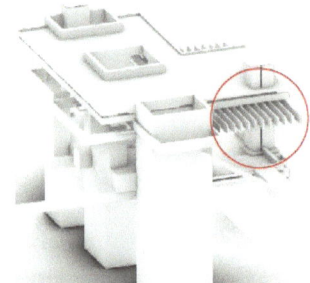

VSA=57°
OP=HP/tanVSA
OP=6.68' or 6'8"
HP=10'6"

East

AIA 2030 PALETTE

Solar Shading

During warm summer months, overhangs block unwanted direct sunlight from solar glazing, reducing cooling loads.

Mountainside Residence

Preventing unnecessary grading of vegetation

Preserving natural drainage patterns

Requiring re-vegetation to maintain the natural landscape environment.

Solar Heat
Wind Flow

ESTIMATED VALUES FOR SINGLE PANE WINDOWS

U = 0.51 BTU/h ft^2
SHGC = 0.52
VLT = 70%
R VALUE = R19

EUI = 21.79 kBTU/sq ft
CO_2 = 13,346.29 lbs

KAPPE

KAPPE RESIDENCE DESIGN PROPOSAL

PROPOSED STRATEGIES
WINDOWS TO TRIPLE-PANE
EXTERIOR INSULATION
CONCRETE FLOOR
SOLAR ENERGY SYSTEM
FAN & FURNACE

SUSTAINABLE CONCEPTS

Proposal
Addition of 30 solar panels
6 kW per 500sf

SOLAR POWER

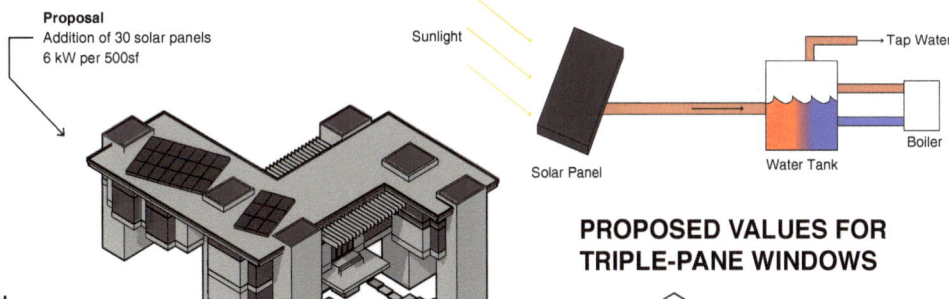

PROPOSED VALUES FOR TRIPLE-PANE WINDOWS

SHGC = 0.21
VLT = 44%

Existing
Single Pane
Wood/Vinyl Frame
U=.52 Btu/h ft^2

Proposed
Clear Argon Triple Pane Low-E
Insulated Fiber Glass/Vinyl Frame
U=.22 Btu/h ft^2

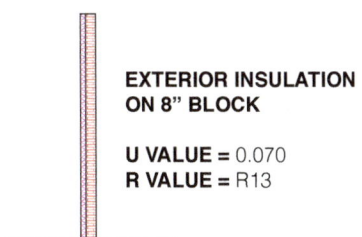

EXTERIOR INSULATION ON 8" BLOCK
U VALUE = 0.070
R VALUE = R13

FAN AND FURNACE

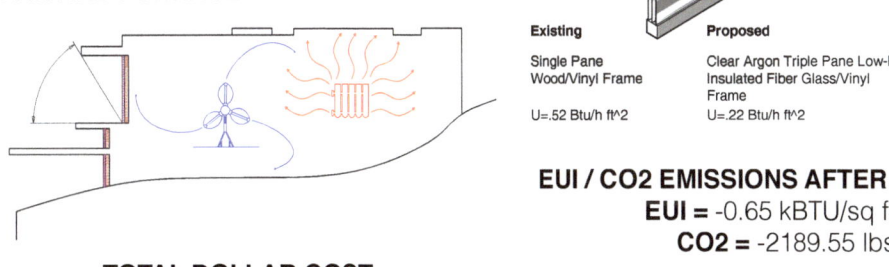

EUI / CO_2 EMISSIONS AFTER:
EUI = -0.65 kBTU/sq ft
CO_2 = -2189.55 lbs

BEPS

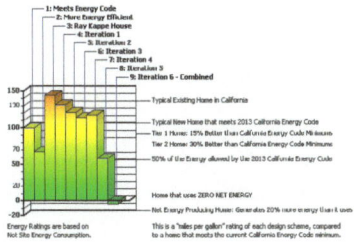

TOTAL DOLLAR COST

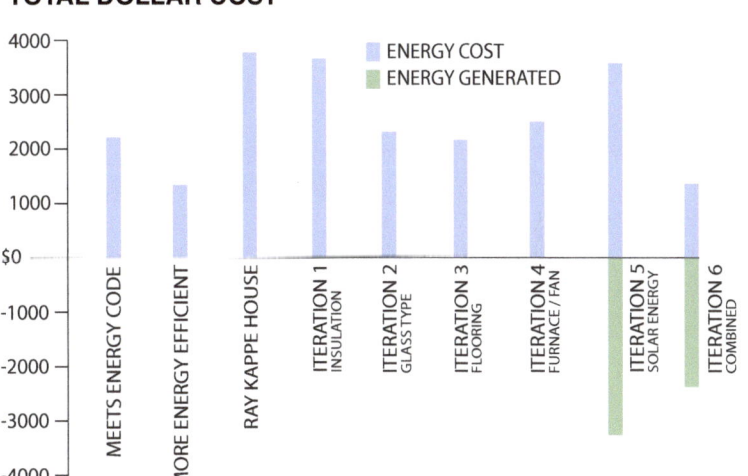

TOTAL ENERGY COST

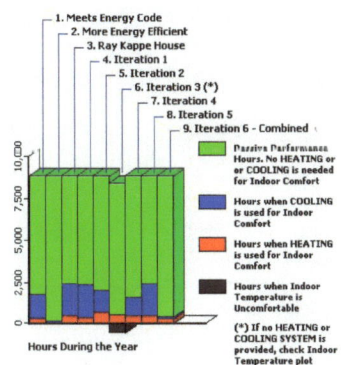

69

Kappe House
City, CA | Architect: Ray Kappe
Group 12: Addy Holenstein, Sarra Starbird, Roman Huante, Zoe Zimmerliny, Ashley Morales

For part 2, HEED was used to make improvements on the original house in order to make it better for the economy as well as a more naturally comfortable environment. We proposed an improvement in shade taken from our analyzation in part one. The original shading device that we analyzed in Part 1 of this project had a required Vertical Shadow Angle (VSA) of thirty degrees, but only exercised one of fifty seven. Since the three primary factors that influence required VSA are the Overhang Projection (OP), the vertical distance from the bottom of the window to the top of the Overhang Projection (HP), and the Orientation of the shading device (NSEW angle), we determined that adjusting the OP from 9'6.5" to 25'4.8" would be the most effective method of achieving a thirty degree VSA because it would be the least invasive to the original design.

We also proposed appropriate climate responsive strategies to improve building performance. In an effort to create a more eco-friendly building, we chose to implement a few climatic responsive strategies to have it become NZE. By using solar panels, you save money and reduce carbon dioxide emissions. By using a thick and glazed pane of glass, thermal efficiency is improved by not allowing outside temperatures affect the inside comfort zone. In addition, by increasing the amount of insulation in the building the home will use less energy for heating, and it will also help regulate the inside temperature. By utilizing interior shading systems, we also increase the amount of natural daylight allowed into the space, creating an overall lower use of energy.

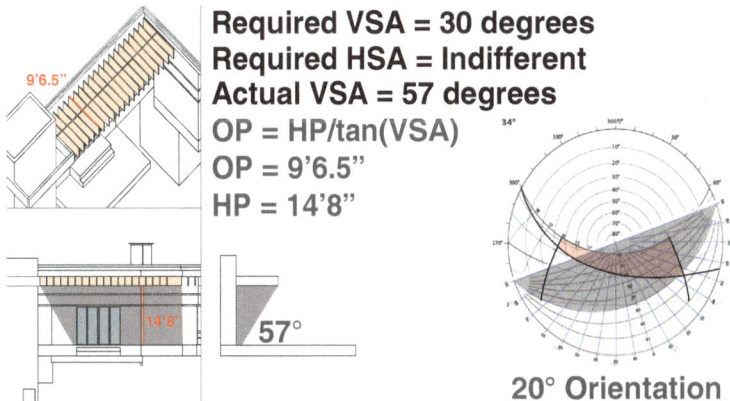

Required VSA = 30 degrees
Required HSA = Indifferent
Actual VSA = 57 degrees
OP = HP/tan(VSA)
OP = 9'6.5"
HP = 14'8"

20° Orientation

KAPPE

Ray Kappe Residence

Net Zero Energy Project // Part 1
Roman Huante, Zoe Zimmerling, Sarra Starbird, Adelaide Holenstein, Ashley Morales

About the project
The Kappe Residence is a project located in the hills of Santa Monica. It's beautiful composition is not only pleasing to the eye, but effectively responsive to the environmental conditions the site presents.

Climate Analysis

Shade:
mid-June - end of October,
8 am - 4 pm

Sun:
mid-June - end of October,
sunrise - 8 am & 4 pm -
sunset
all day from November -
mid-June.

Overheated and Underheated Periods

Dry Bulb Temp. During Time and Month | Distance from the House to Weather Station
Tempature Range During the Year | Psychrometric Chart and Energy Strategy

Existing Shading Device Analysis

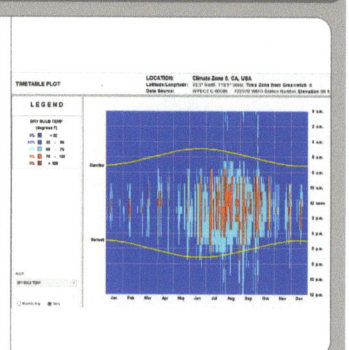

Required VSA = 30 degrees
Required HSA = Indifferent
Actual VSA = 57 degrees
OP = HP/tan(VSA)
OP = 9'6.5"
HP = 14'8"

20° Orientation

Response to Climate

Wind — Cross Ventilation
Columns — Thermal Mass
Overhangs — Shade
Trees — Variable Shade

Bioclimatic Strategies

Example of Cross Ventilation
Morerava Cottages, AATA Arquitectos
Hanga Roa, Easter Island, Chile

Example of top daylighting
New Headquarters of a Financial Company
Philippe Samyn and Partners
Gerpinnes, Belgium

Example of Direct Gain: Glazing
Rocky Mountain Institute
ZGF Architects
Basalt, Colorado, United States

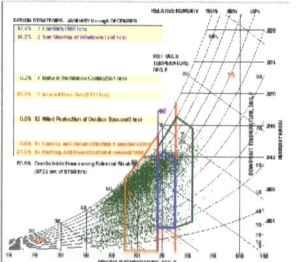

1. Natural Ventilation
2. Fan Forced Ventilation Cooling
3. Internal Heat Gain
4. Wind Protection of Outdoor Spaces
5. Cooling, add Dehumidification if needed
6. Heating, add Humidification if needed

Ray Kappe Residence

Net Zero Energy Project // Part 2
Roman Huante, Zoe Zimmerling, Sarra Starbird, Adelaide Holenstein, Ashley Morales

KAPPE

About the project
The Kappe Residence is a project located in the hills of Santa Monica. It's beautiful composition is not only pleasing to the eye, but effectively responsive to the environmental conditions the site presents.

Performance Metrics

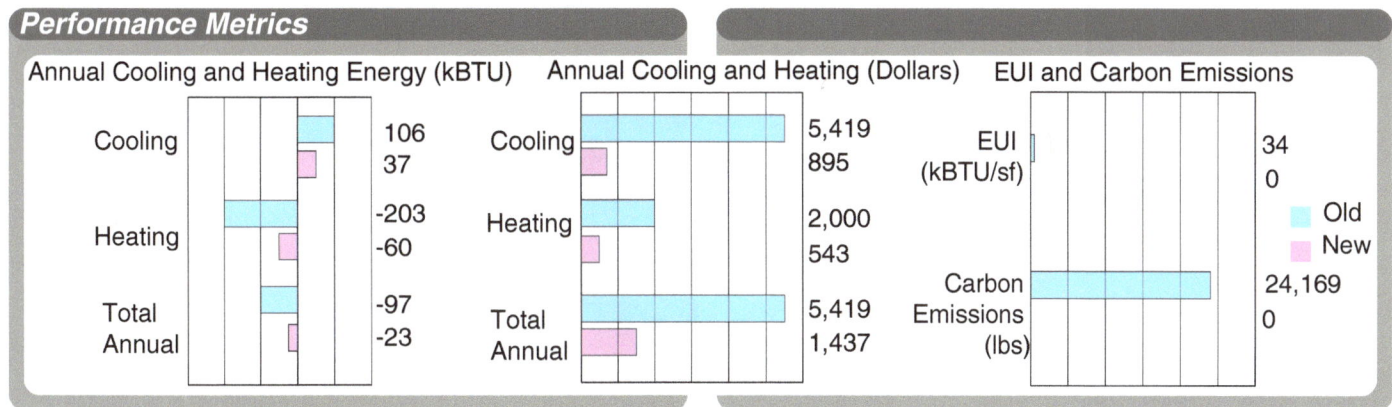

Improved Shading Device Analysis

Required VSA = 30 degrees
Required HSA = Indifferent
Improved VSA = 30 degrees
OP = HP/tan(VSA)
New OP = 25'4.8"
HP = 14'8"

30°
20° Orientation

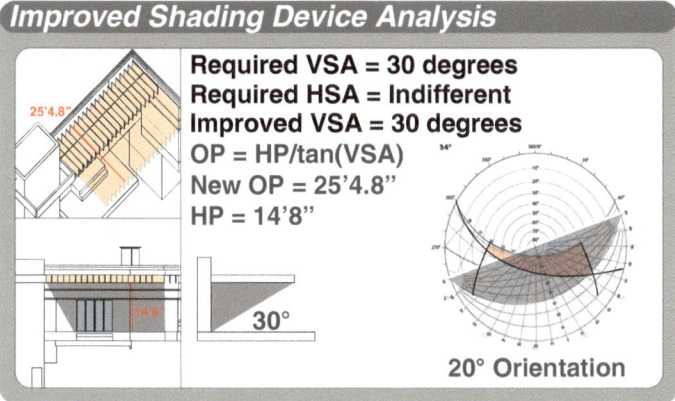

Sustainable Concept Diagram

Solar Panels
Glazed Windows
Interior Shading: Mesh Screens

Carbon Emission = 0
EUI = 0
30 Solar Panels

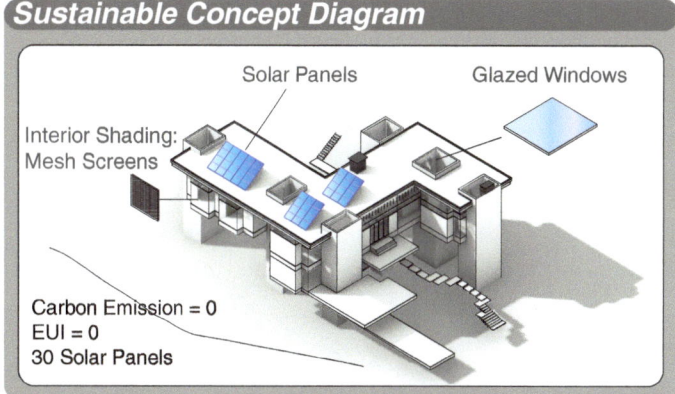

Climate Responsive Strategies

IMPROVED MECHANICAL SYSTEMS

A. Solar Panels (30)
B. Increase in insulation
C. Higher Performing tripple pane (Glazed) Windows with interior shading system (Mesh Screens)

Original R Value = 0.90
New R Value = 4.35

U Value = 0.23
SHGC = 0.22
22% of solar heat transmitted
VLT = 0.65
65% of visible light transmitted

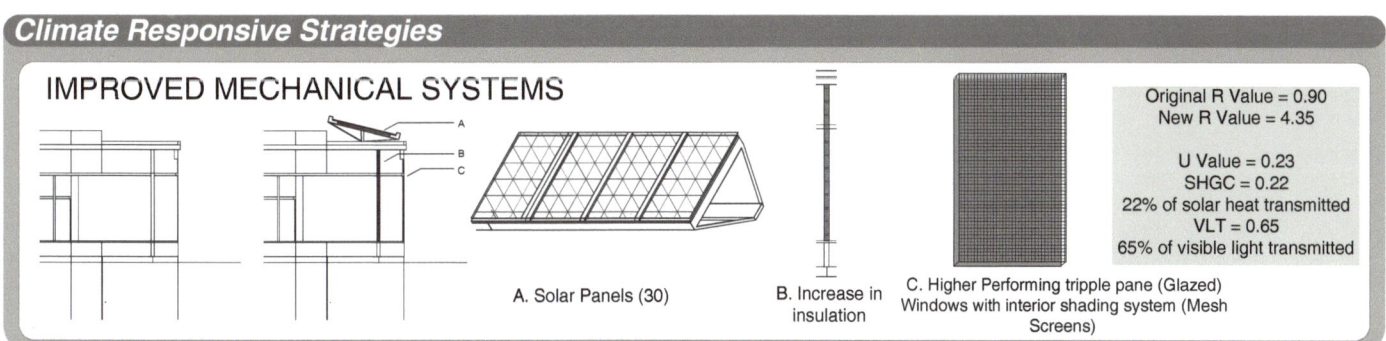

Kappe House

City, CA | Architect: Ray Kappe
Group 13: Peyra Rodriguez, Valeria Redekosky, Brarolice Reza, Marc Mendez, Ashy Saucedo

Sustainable design and climate responsive features are what make architecture that has a low energy impact on the environment and is able to sustain itself through means of just design instead of using energy-driven products. In the design of the Ray Kappe House there are sustainable design and climate responsive feature found around the house. There are various levels that are all intermittently connected with an open and free lowing design that provides a great deal of cross-ventilation. This cross-ventilation maintains the house within the comfort zone for most part of the day. The house is also given natural lighting by means of large glass windows, skylights, mitered corner windows, and clerestories. Other means of creating shade throughout the more warmer times are by the chosen materials around the house. Concrete aids in regulating human comfort and another more particular design which creates shading are the overhangs and the trellises that are designed from the wooden beams.

Description of Proposed Sustainable Strategies:

While the Raye Kappe House is located in California which tends to have a hotter climate, it is surrounded by trees. This influx of shade helps with the hot days and allows for ventilation and cooler temperatures in the interior of the house, but when the cold months appear, or even the drop in temperature overnight, it is difficult to heat a space. This is why implementing these four design strategies would help allow the space to conserve or absorb some heat for when temperatures drop. Shortening the overhang that is located on two sides of the house will allow for more light to bleed into the large doors and windows beneath it. In addition to this, changing the windows from one pane to double paned glass would allow for the absorption and insulation to help contain the heat in when the temperature drops outside. This also goes with the insulation being added in the walls, which would also maintain the heat inside the building longer. The last strategy implemented in the house to help with the cool temperatures is the roof pond. This will not only allow for more solar radiation absorption to heat the house when its cold outside, but also the opposite effect, which would be to cool the house when its hot outside.

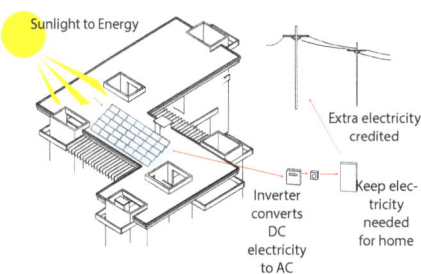

KAPPE

Ray Kappe House
Architect: Ray Kappe
Group: 11

ARC3310.01 Environmental Controls System

The weather information that is recorded for the zone where the Raye Kappe House is located is at the Santa Monica Airport. This map shows where they are located in relation to each other.

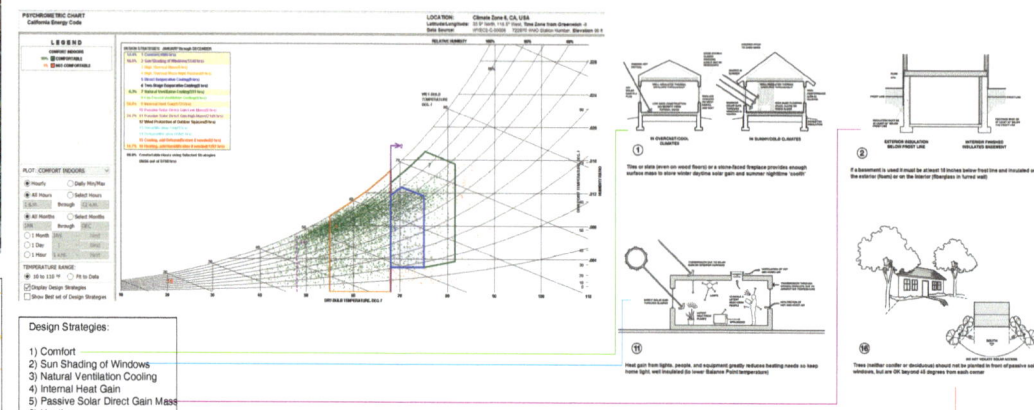

Design Strategies:
1) Comfort
2) Sun Shading of Windows
3) Natural Ventilation Cooling
4) Internal Heat Gain
5) Passive Solar Direct Gain Mass
6) Heating

There are 4 design strategies that are represented by the diagrams, these design strategies allow the comfort zone to be exactly 100%.

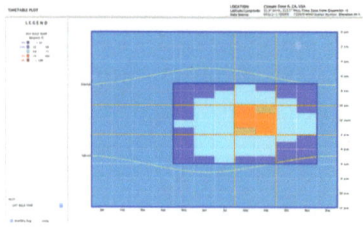

The overheated periods for the Raye Kappe House are during the months of August and September between 10:00 am and 2:00 pm. The underheated periods for the Raye Kappe House are experienced year-round, but felt most in Dec.- April.

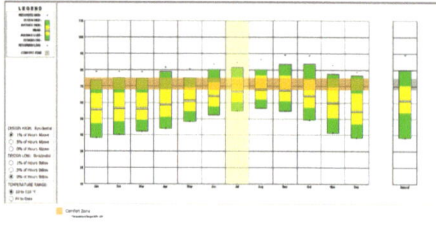

The temperature range chart shows the comfort zone in the area where the building is located(orange). It also shows how in July, the mean temperature is perfectly in the comfort zone.

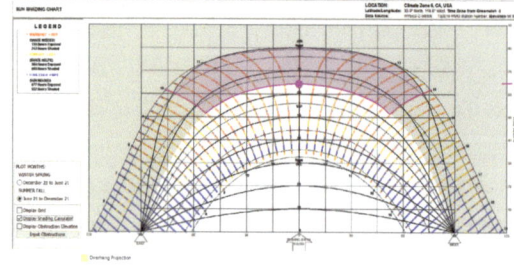

The sun shading chart shows the area that is shaded by the overhang (pink). This shows that from mid July to September, the overhang is shading the space completely.

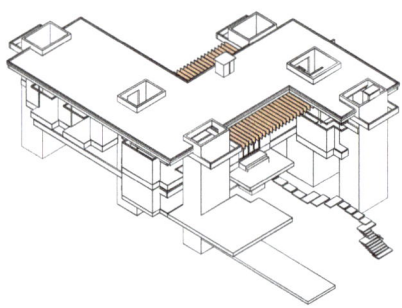

The sustainability feature focused on was the overhang shading over a door. The overhang is long enough to provide shade in the interior of the house with these windows and doors. In addition to shade, it allows the space to stay cooled rather than warm when the beaming sun shines on it.

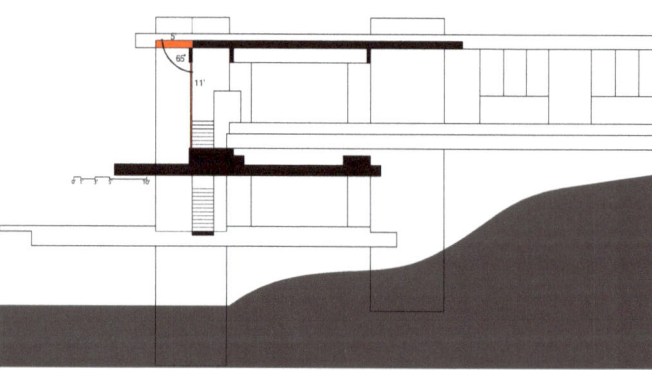

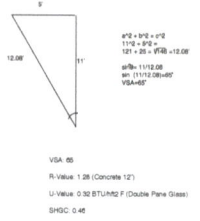

VSA: 65
R-Value: 1.28 (Concrete 12")
U-Value: 0.32 BTU/ft2-F (Double Pane Glass)
SHGC: 0.46

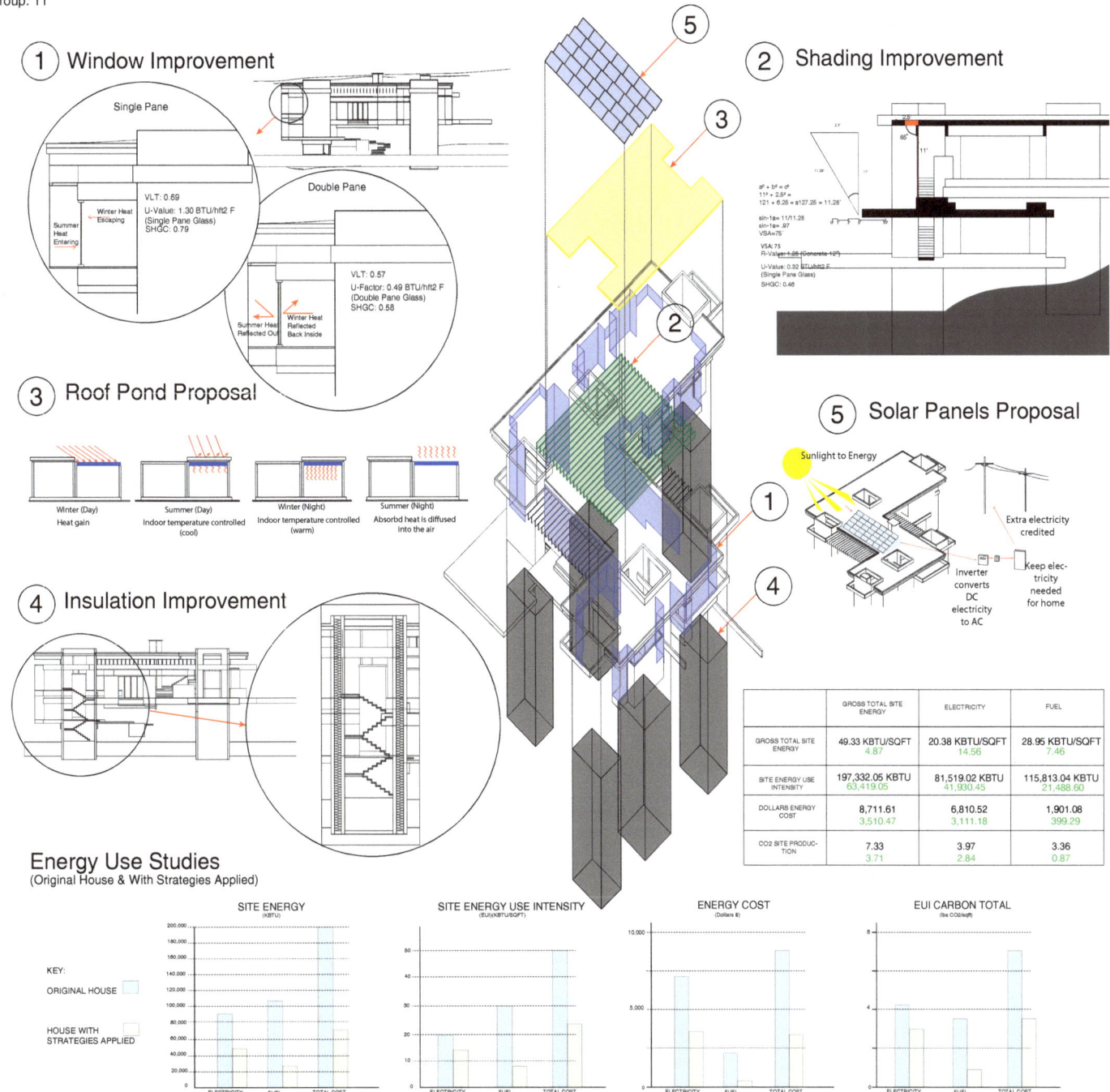

Kappe House
City, CA | Architect: Ray Kappe
Group 14: Sidra Issa, Alex Menjivar, Jaylene Sanchez, Christian Serrano, Anne Marie Jao

The Ray Kappe Residence is located in Santa Monica climate zone 6. The weather station SCE Topanga Canyon is approximately 5.5 miles away from the Kappe residence. The climate here is mostly coastal and warm year round. About 80% of the year the relative humidity is kept above 60% and over half of this 60% is above 80% humidity. Although there are nuances where the humidity drops to 20% it is insignificant because it is about 2% of the time.

Throughout the year there is always a portion of the temperature which is under the thermal comfort level. This gives the kappe house and advantage because it is either at comfort level or very close to it.

The strategies we will be using based on the psychometric chart will be natural ventilation which contributes to 6.3% of comfort levels, Internal heat gain which contributes 58.6% and passive solar direct gain high mass which is 24.7%. The remaining 14.7% will be made up with the addition of heating unit.

Indoor comfort is an essential part of the Ray Kappe house's function, features that help characterize it as an energy saving home. Through the use of cross-ventilation the home makes it easy for the wind cooling systems installed to naturally cool interior.
U Factor determined to be 1.30= amount of heat transmission through the building part
Insulations is minimal if not non-existent.

The trees and slope of the landscape allow for maximum aid in the combating of cold winds during the winter season. On the other hand, the deciduous trees also play another energy saving role when their leaves fall in the wall maximizing solar heat gain through the southeast glass doors that penetrate with solar radiation. The single-glazed clear window paneling invites a SHGC of about 0.79, amounting to a VRT of 0.69.

The Ray Kappe Residence is facing east. Rooms that are located on the east side of the house usually gain their heat in the morning and it will be cool by the evening. This can help during the summer, as the temperature will be cooler in the evening and will make it comfortable for sleeping.

With the aid of the horizontal sun shading projection, it is possible to graph the point and be able to understand what time it will provide shade and for how long. Although there is already shading it is very minimal so we plan on remodeling this feature into a controllable cover to fully shade the area when needed. The whole house fan reduces the amount of CO_2 which is being produced by the house from 14,479 lbs to 8,876.92 lbs. Solar Panels will reduce the energy cost from $6,130 to $2,060.

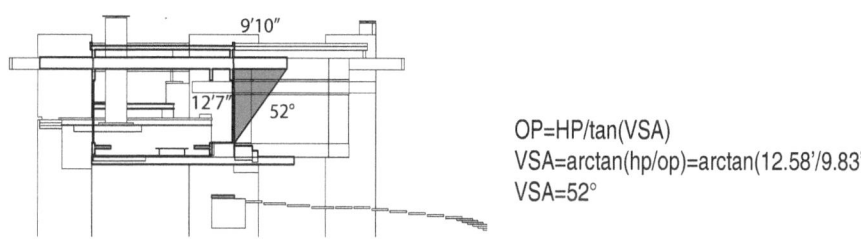

OP=HP/tan(VSA)
VSA=arctan(hp/op)=arctan(12.58'/9.83')
VSA=52°

KAPPE

Ray Kappe House
Climate and Building Analysis

CLIMATE ZONE

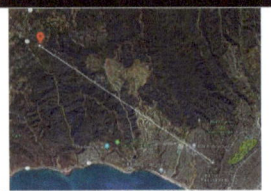

1. The Ray Kappe Residence is located in climate zone 6.

2. About 80% of the year the relative humidity is kept above 60% and over half of this 60% is above 80% humidity.

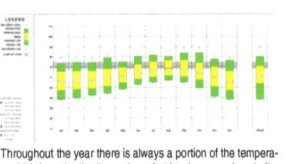

3. Throughout the year there is always a portion of the temperature which is under the thermal comfort level or very close to it.

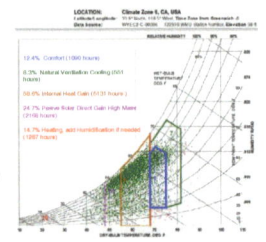

4. The strategies we will be using based on the psychrometric chart will be natural ventilation Internal heat gain and passive solar direct gain high mass. The remaining will be made up with the addition of solar panels.v

Through the use of cross-ventilation the home makes it easy for the wind cooling systems installed to naturally cool interior.

U Factor determined to be 1.30= amount of heat transmision through the building part

Insulations is minimal if not non-existent.

The trees and slope of the landscape allow for maximum aid in the combating of cold winds during the winter season.

On the other hand, the decidious trees also play another energy saving role when their leaves fall in the wall maximizing solar heat gain through the southeast glass doors that penetrate with solar radiation.

The single-glazed clear window paneling invites a SHGC of about 0.79, amounting to a VRT of 0.69.

BIOCLIMATIC STRATEGIES

Solar Shading
During the summer, overhangs can block direct sunlight which reduces unwanted heat.

Glazing
Solar glazing on windows allows direct sunlight to enter a space for passive heating in the winter.

Night Vent Cooling
Thermal masses like concrete and masonry that are located in a space and cooled at night absorb heat and create a cool indoor space. The larger the surface area of the mass, the more stable the temperature will be.

EXISTING SHADE

The Ray Kappe Residence is facing east. Rooms that are located on the east side of the house usually gain their heat in the morning and it will be cool by the evening. This can help during the summer, as the temperature will be cooler in the evening and will make it comfortable for sleeping.

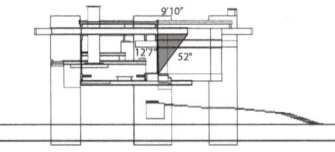

OP=HP/tan(VSA)
VSA=arctan(hp/op)=arctan(12.58'/9.83')
VSA=52°

OVERHEATED AND UNDERHEATED PERIODS

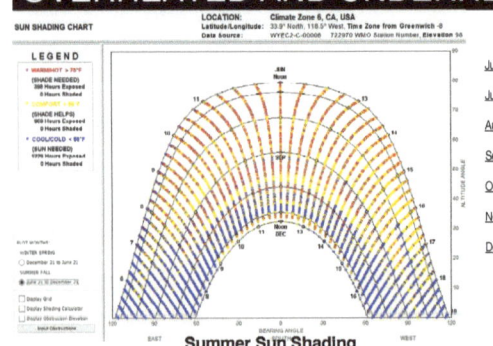

Shade Needed
June 10am-6pm
July 7am-9pm
August 9am-6pm
September 7am-5:30pm
October 9am-4:30pm
November 9am-6pm
December 9am-6pm

Summer Sun Shading

Sun Needed
December 8am-4pm
January 8am-4pm
February 8am-4pm
March 8am-6pm
April 6am-6pm
May 6am-10am / 4pm-6pm
June 6am-10am / 4pm-6pm

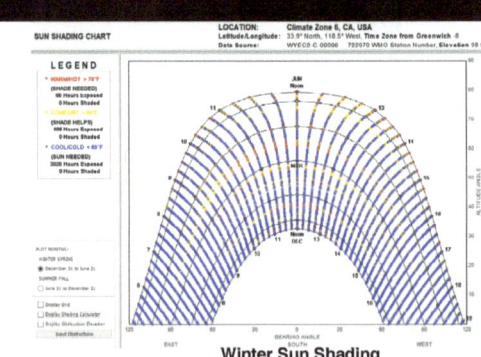

Winter Sun Shading

KAPPE

DESIGN PROPOSALS

SOLAR SHADING

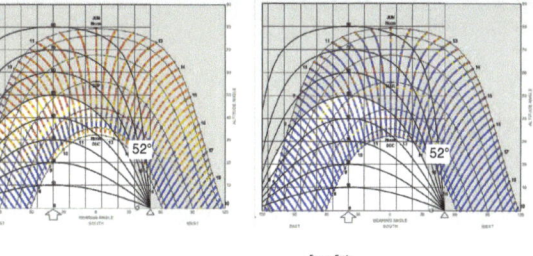

Although there is already shading it is very minimal so we plan on remodeling this feature into a controlable cover to fully shade the area when needed.

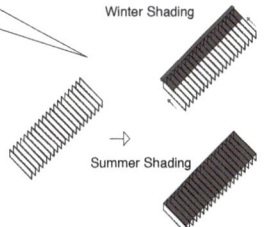

Winter Shading

Summer Shading

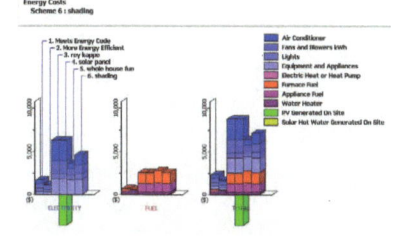

SOLAR PANELS

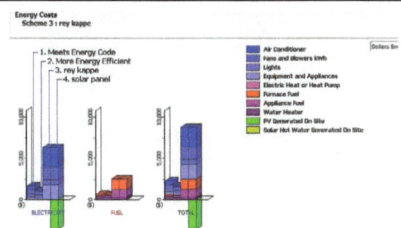

Solar Panels will reduce the energy cost from $6,1230 to $2,060

WHOLE HOUSE FAN

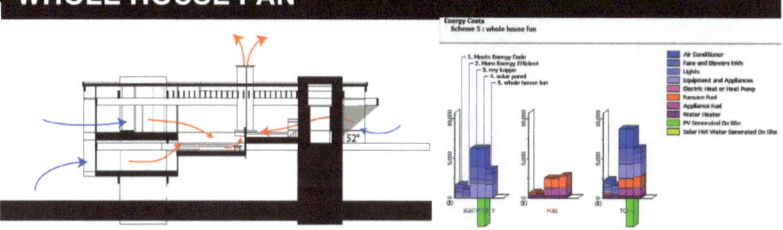

The whole house fans reduces the amount of CO2 which is being produced by the house from 14,479 lbs to 8,876.92 lbs

Before solar panels

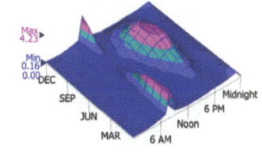

After solar panels

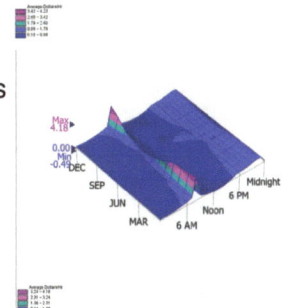

COMBINED PROPOSED RESULTS

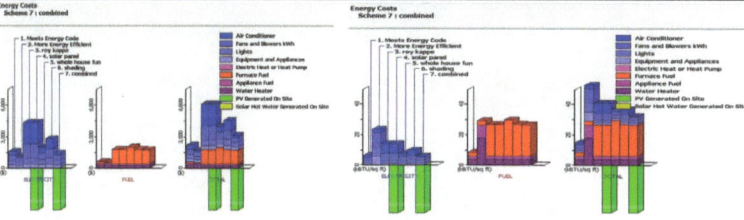

Annual energy costs   Annual kBTU consumption

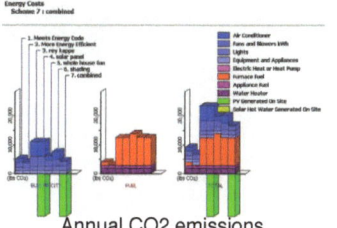

Annual CO2 emissions

The overall outcome of the Ray Kappe house cost analysis reduced from an annual total of $5,945.98 to $517.13 Both the EUI and the CO2 production levels resulted in net zero emissions.

CO2 Original: 22,56259lbs
CO2 New: -234.3 lbs

EUI Original: 39.42 kBTU
EUI New: -5.36 kBTU

King's Road House
City, CA | Architect: Rudolf Schindler

King's Road House

City, CA | Architect: Rudolf Schindler
Group 15: Noah Lum, Lorenzo Tayag, Ivanah Sagabaen Palagarias, Yaozhen Liu, Daniel Alejandro Aguilera

The house we have decided to remodel as net zero energy is the Rudolph Schindler's King's Road House. The house resides in Climate Zone Number 9, which has warmer summers and cool winters compared to the coastal zones of California. The house already has a light colored roof which can reflect a lot of the sunlight since the King's Road House is located in the urban area of Los Angeles. The cool roof helps reduce the overheated condition, and will reduce the energy usage because the air conditioner is being used less often. In addition, it improves the comfort in rooms which are not air conditioned.

In order to reach Net Zero Energy, we have decided to elongate the sun shading devices on the South side so that the windows will stay under the shade later into the day, reducing direct sunlight. In the northern hemisphere, we obtain the most amount of sun on the south side, thus we can maximize the amount of energy we let in as heat by shading that side. We have also raised the house's view deck in order to increase ventilation of the structure in order to keep cooler in the hot summers. This allows for more hot air to rise and escape the room.

Sustainable Concept Diagram

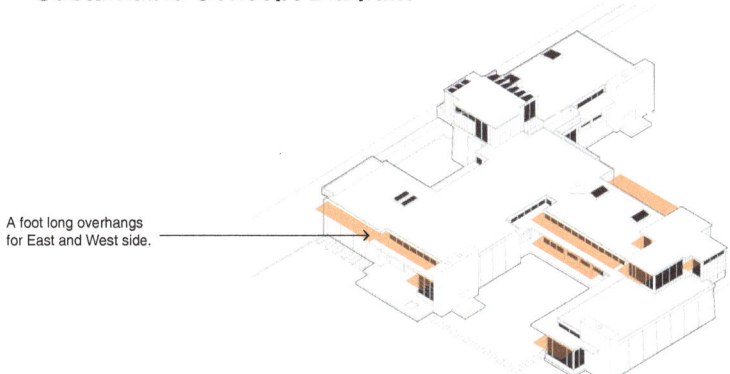

KING'S ROAD

Schindler House
Climate Analysis

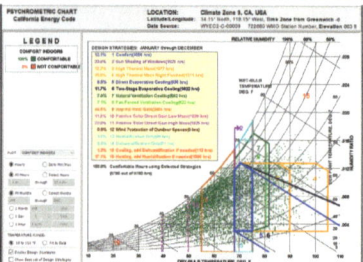

The Shchindler House is located on 833 N Kings Rd, West Hollywood, CA. The climate zone for Los Angeles is climate zone number 9. Summers are generally warmer and winters are generally cooler compared to the coast. The amount of daylit hours and solar radiation is lower on average during the winters and higher on average during the summers. The least humidity would occur around October while the most humid days are between July and

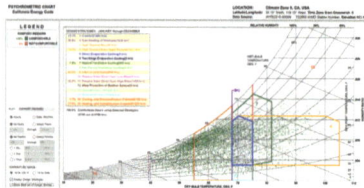

Recommended Strategies (Climate Consultant)

- Sun Shading of Windows
- High Thermal Mass Night Flushed
- Natural Ventilation
- Internal Heat Gain
- Passive Solar Direct Gain High Mass
- Cooling, and Dehumidification if needed
- Heating, add Humidifcation if needed

Case Studies w/ Similar Strategies (2030 Pallette)

-For passive solar heating, face most of the glass area south to maximize winter sun exposure and design overhangs to fully shade in summer
    -Example: Rocky Mountain Institute (ZGF Architects)

-Flat roofs work well in hot dry climates (especially if light colored)
    -Example: Olso Opera House (Snøhetta)

-Organize floorplan so winter sun penetrates into daytime use spaces witt specific functions that coincide with solar orientation
    -The Village, Watergate Bay (Architects Design Group)

The WMO station number is 722880 and is located in Burbank/Glendale. It's roughly 9.5 miles away from the Schindler

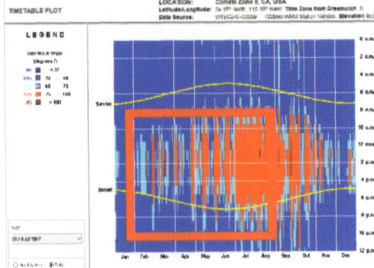

According to the Timetable Plot, The overheated months are form Feburary to November, mostly from 8am to 7:30pm.

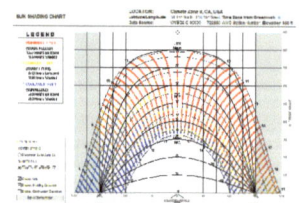

According to the Sun shading chart, from December 21st to Jun 21st, the King's Road House needs to be shaded from 9am to 15:30pm; the sun is needed from 6am to 8am and from 16:00pm to 19:00pm.

According to the Sun shading chart, from Jun 21st to December 21st, the King's Road House needs to be shaded from 8am to 15:30pm; the sun is needed from 6am to 7am.

According to the 2030 palette , in hot climates, and climates with hot summers, a light color roof reflects sun lights, and it can offset CO_2 warming, and reduces the amount of heat transferred to the interior of the house.

As the King's road house is located at the urban area of Los Angles, the cool roof can reduce the overheated condition. Also, it can improve indoor comfort to spaces that are not air conditioned, such as garage or covered patio. Cool light-colored roof reduces air-conditioning use during **the day's hottest period so that it** reduces the costs on the energy.

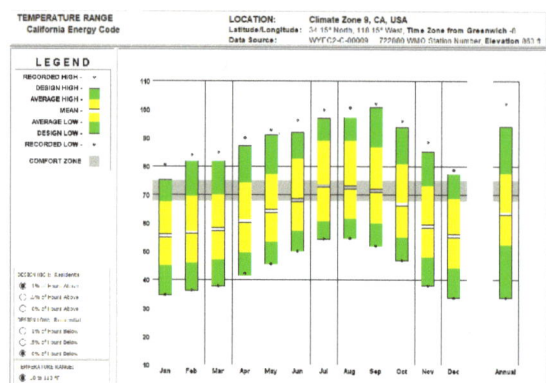

The temperatures during the months June through September sit much higher than the other months above the comfort level. December through March stays much cooler, and only warms a little during peak sun hours.

Shading and Site Analysis:

Schindler House
Design Proposal

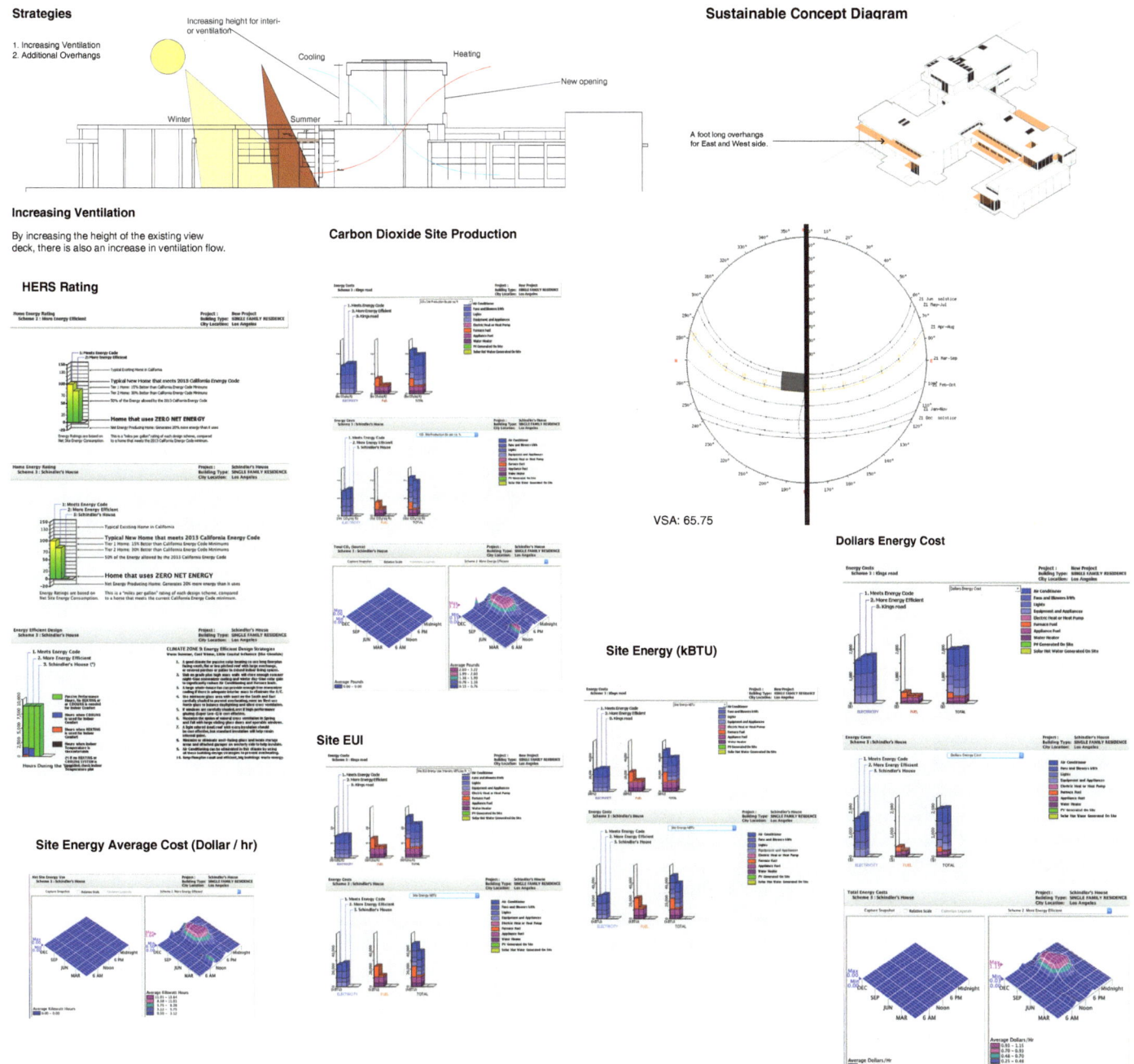

King's Road House
City, CA | Architect: Rudolf Schindler
Group 16: Carl Arnesto, Daniel Vasquez, Sandee Deogaygay, Khoi Van

History : Rudolf Schindler's King's Road House was designed in 1921 and completed in 1922. Schindler did not originally intend for the house to be a single-family residence for him and his wife, but to be shared with Marian and Clyde Chase. The house consists of what Schindler refers to as individual studios and communal spaces. The house was designed around the idea of two young couples living within it. Each adult would have their own private space and each couple would have access to their own bathroom and patio, the roof terraces, and a communal kitchen. The material used to build the house consisted of concrete, glass, lumber, and canvas. The house had a view of the garden surrounding it from almost every room. After Schindler's death, his ex-wife Pauline created the nonprofit "Friends of the Schindler House" to preserve the house. It is not the MAK Center for Art and Architecture and is used as a public gallery in West Hollywood.

Climate: The climate where the King's Road House is located has the luxury of having both a coastal climate and a more inland climate. In the hotter months (July and August) the temperature on average is around 60 to 90 degrees Fahrenheit, while during the cooler months (January and December) the temperature is around 45 to 70 degrees Fahrenheit. West Hollywood does not get as much rainfall as other places in the U.S. with about 14 inches of rainfall a year, but during the colder months it is noticeably more wet than its hotter months where it is significantly dryer.

Existing Comfort: King's Road House has a few qualities that contribute to climate and comfort of those who used to reside in it. The house contains many windows. The abundance of windows allows a great amount of natural light within the residence as well as give the residents views of the surrounding garden regardless of the room they are in. There are also roof terraces that also act as sleeping areas. With the Los Angeles climate one would be able to sleep comfortably on the roof terrace sleeping area without getting too hot or cold, especially with the amount of foliage around the area.

Proposed Design: The proposed idea consists of using white gravel to allow reflectivity on the rooftop allowing for a cool roof to be activated. We also Implemented an operable window design into the house allowing for greater natural ventilation and as well as night flushing allowing for a more comfortable night. Using a concrete roof amplifies the high thermal massing allowing for greater night flushing. To allow fresher air into the site, a vegetative wall was designed to allow for a Co2 absorption and cleaner air. Slab on grade has been extended to allow for more heat to absorb into the ground allowing more heat mass. Double pane argon gas filed windows have been implemented into the design to allow for a more significant polar solar gain. A high reflective coating is then finished on the roof creating a cooler roof by reducing heat absorption.

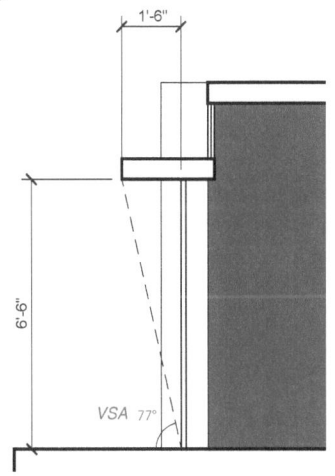

VSA=arcTan(*6'-6"/1'-6"*)
VSA=77   **HSA**= 0

KING'S ROAD HOUSE

OVERHEATED AND UNDERHEATED PERIODS

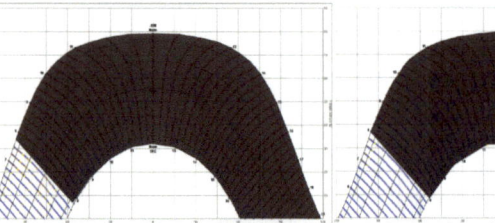

Hours and dates needed to be shaded:
449 hours from December 21 to June 21
1193 hours from June 21 to December 21
Hours and dates needed sunlight:
1519 hours from December 21 to June 21
872 hours from June 21 to December 21

Months that needed shading:
July to August
Months needed sun lights:
December to January

SHADE DESIGN

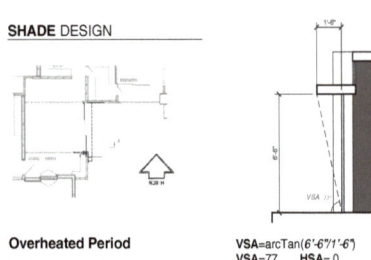

Overheated Period

Shadow Mask

VSA=arcTan(6'-6"/1'-6")
VSA=77   HSA= 0

Because of the building's parallel orientation to the north, this overhang serves to shade the Eastern entry/exit located on the perimeter of the residence. As the diagram below shows, it shades around 70% of the Overheated period.

BIOCLIMATIC STRATEGIES

INDIRECT GAIN: SUNSPACE

DIRECT GAIN: HEAT STORAGE

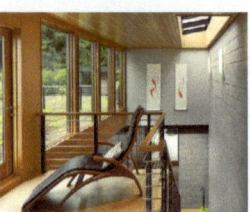

COOL ROOF

2030 Palette Examples:
Indirect Gain: Sunspace
Cool Roof
Direct Gain Heat Storage

DESCRIPTION

Kings Road House focuses on using natural ventilation to create a suitable design through hot and cold climates. The use of the shaded outdoor spaces such as courtyards extend living spaces. Ceiling fans or outdoor motion can lower indoor temperatures by 5 degrees and reduce the use of air conditioning. Creating overhangs or operable sunshades can reduce or even eliminate the use of air conditioning. The use of good natural ventilation allows the house to eliminate air conditioning in warm weather, if windows are shaded and placed in an area receiving prevailing breezes

RESPONSE TO CLIMATE

Provide double pane high performance glazing (Low-E) on west, north, and east, but clear on south for maximum passive solar gain

This is one of the more comfortable climates, so shade to prevent overheating, open to breezes in summer, and use passive solar gain in winter

best high mass walls use exterior insulation (like EIFS foam) and expose the ...us on the interior or add plaster or direct contact drywall

A whole-house fan or natural ventilation can store nighttime 'coolth' in high mass interior surfaces (night flushing), to reduce or eliminate air conditioning

NZE PROJECT: Kingsroad House

Group 13: Khoi Van, Sandee Deogaygay, Carl Arnesto, Daniel Vazquez

KING'S ROAD

Corresponding Strategies

Form for Heating: A building form with ample surface area exposed to direct sunlight in winter can easily incorporate passive heating systems.

Direct Gain Glazing: Solar glazing admits direct sunlight into a space for passive heating in winter. Solar glazing (facing the equator) is sized to admit enough sunlight on an average sunny winter day to heat a space over the full 24-hour period.

Direct Gain Heat Storage: Thermal mass – masonry floors, walls and/or ceilings – absorb and store daytime solar heat in winter for release at night.

Cool Roof: Cool roofs have surfaces that reflect sunlight and emit or discharge heat efficiently, keeping them cooler on sunny days. The two surface properties that determine a roof's temperature are solar reflectance and thermal emittance, which range on a scale from 0 to 1. The larger the two values are, the cooler the roof will be.

Natural Ventilation: Window openings located perpendicular to prevailing winds, and coupled with openings on the opposite side of a space or building, will provide natural ventilation for fresh air and/or space cooling. Adequate cross ventilation will remove heat from a space or building and maintain indoor air temperatures approximately 1.5 C° (2.7 F°) above the outdoor air temperatures.

Performance Metrics

CO_2	Lb/ft2
Gross	5.11 lbs/ft2
Net	5.11 lbs/ft²
Gross (Proposed)	1.93 lbs/ft2
Net (Proposed)	-0.65
Electric Value	**Dollars**
Gross	901.26
Net	901.26
Gross (Proposed)	1896.09
Net (Proposed)	-1200.16
Fuel Value	**Dollars**
Gross	1928.65
Net	1928.65
Gross (Proposed)	222.14
Net (Proposed)	222.14
Total Value	**Dollars**
Gross	2829.92
Net	2829.92
Gross (Proposed)	2118.23
Net (Proposed)	-978.02
Electric Site Energy	**kBTU/sqft**
Gross	5
Net	5
Gross (Proposed)	8.11
Net (Proposed)	-5.13
Fuel Site Energy	**kBTU/sqft**
Gross	35.31
Net	35.31
Gross (Proposed)	2.99
Net (Proposed)	2.99
Total Site Energy	**kBTU/sqft**
Gross	40.31
Net	40.31
Gross (Proposed)	11.1
Net (Proposed)	-2.14
Total Site Energy	**kBTU**
Gross	
Net	
Gross (Proposed)	38904.31
Net (Proposed)	-7514.81

PROJECT	ENERGY (kBTU)	COST
Original Desig	141,242.00	$2,829.92
w/ Insulation	38,496	$1,106.78
w/ Electrical I	32,753	$1,553.57
w/ 35 PV Pan	32,753	($1,264.54)

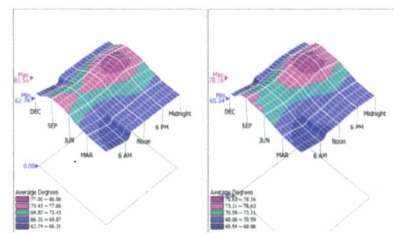

Improvement of around 2 degrees on both minimum and maximun indoor temperature

- Absorbtion of heat by concrete slab acting as thermal mass
- Times of day where current orientation generates most energy

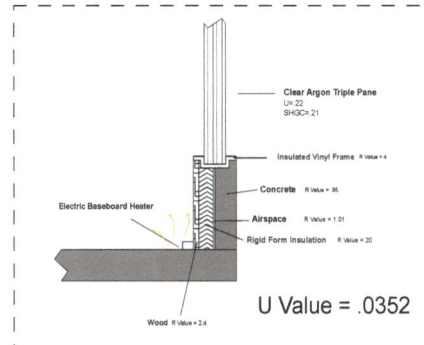

U Value = .0352

Strategy Implementation

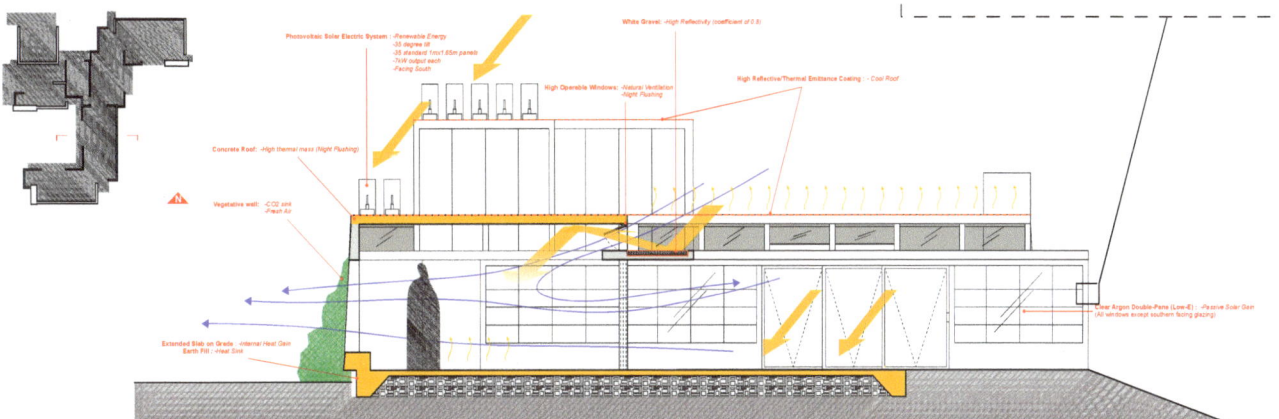

King's Road House
City, CA | Architect: Rudolf Schindler
Group 17: Brian Caballero, Juan Garcia, Michael Hernandez, Emanuel Cardenas, Ivonne Murillo

    In this project, we made some investigations and went over why the schendlier house became an iconic piece of architect through its climate responsive techniques. For example, the house has installed overhangs facing southern sun exposure which allows it to be the most flexible when controlling the sun. By having just an overhang at the correct height and length, then the overhang would allow sun in the winter and block sun when it's in the hot summer. Furthermore, the house also shows how the architect uses an open floorplan which allows cross ventilation to ventilation to occur. By having a house to have cross ventilation floorplan you can allow natural ventilation and night flush to occur, in which would you house to cool the temperature drastically.

In addition, after reviewing the list of cooling techniques that the house contains, with today's tools and knowledge we would like to introduce new techniques in which will allow the house to be net zero, such as the house can maintain itself without any machine effort. The list starts with glaze windows, evaporative cooling, and white roof. Evaporative cooling would have several branches from it, for example if we can add a pool in between the courtyard then it lowers the ambient temperature. Others would be having small ponds or misters around the edge of the house. Since the temperature in climate zone 9 mainly dry then this allows air to evaporate in the hot summer. Having a white roof would allow the sun to reflect, so then the building doesn't absorb as much heat gain if it was a normal color where the sun doesn't reflect.

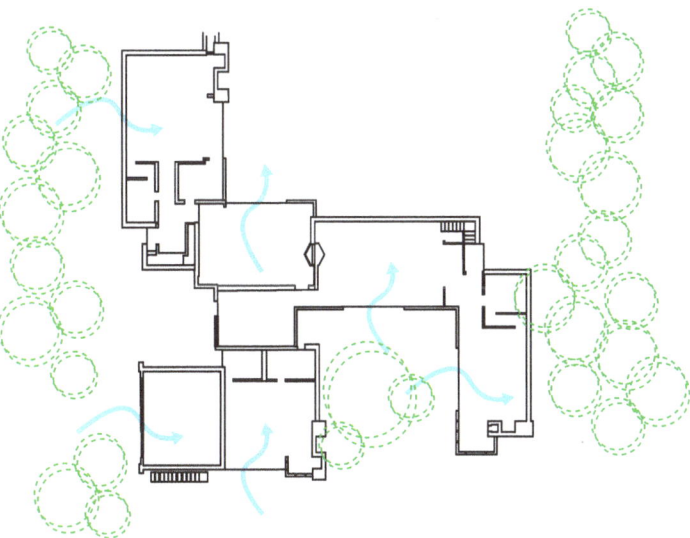

KING'S ROAD

Climate and Building Analysis / Kings Road House / Rudolf Schindler

Climate Analysis

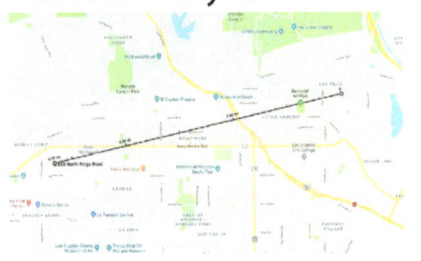

Map (Figure 1.1)

Location: 833 N Kings Rd, West Hollywood, CA 90069

Weather Station: 3151 Prospect Ave, Los Angeles, CA 90027

Temperature Range (Figure 1.2)

Average High: -88F
Average Low: -45F

Timetable Plot (Figure 1.3)

Recommended Strategies

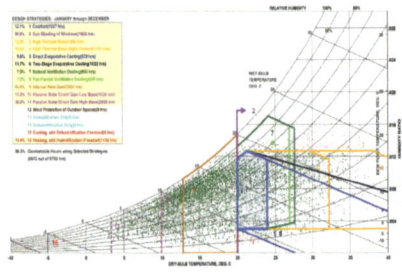 

Psychometric Chart (Figure 1.6)

Direct Gain: Glazing
Rocky Mountain Institute; ZGF Architects; Basalt, Colorado, United States; Credit: Tim Griffith

Cool Roof

Von Karman Corporate Center; Irvine, California, United States; Credit: DRI Commercial

Solar Shading
Edward Gonzales Elementary School; Mazria Oderns Dzurec Architects; Albuquerque, New Mexico, United States; Credit: Mazria, Inc

Night Vent Cooling

Germantown Friends School; SMP Architects; Philadelphia, Pennsylvania, United States; Credit: Barry Halkin Photography

Earth Sheltering

Buried Home; Parame, Saint-Malo, France; Credit: John Leather via Flickr

Indirect Gain: Sunspace
Vieider House; Egger-Aichner-Seidl; Valdaora de Sopra, Bolzano, Italy; Credit: Rossano Albatici

©2030 Pallette

Existing Shade

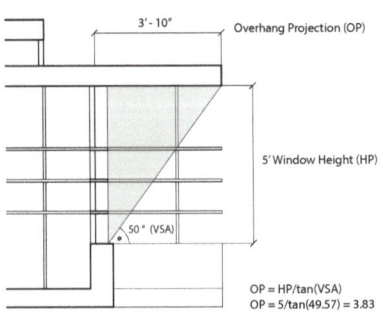

Window Overhang Section (Figure 1.4)

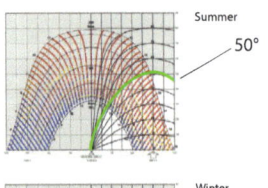
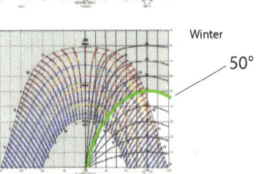

Sun Path Diagrams (Figure 1.5)

Original Strategies

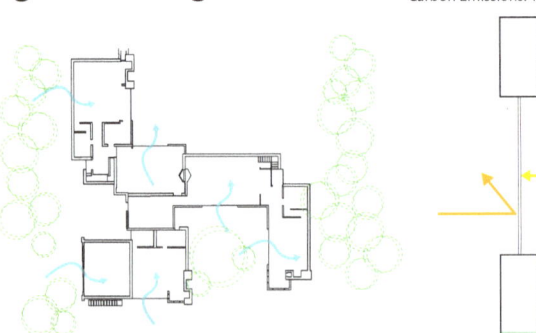

Air Ventilation (Figure 1.7)

EUI: 10.97 kBTU/sq.ft
Carbon Emissions: 1.91 lbs per sq.ft

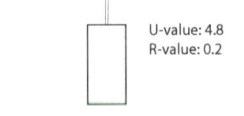

U-value: 4.8
R-value: 0.2

Window Glazing (Figure 1.8)

Design Proposal / Kings Road House / Rudolf Schindler

Sustainable Concept Diagram

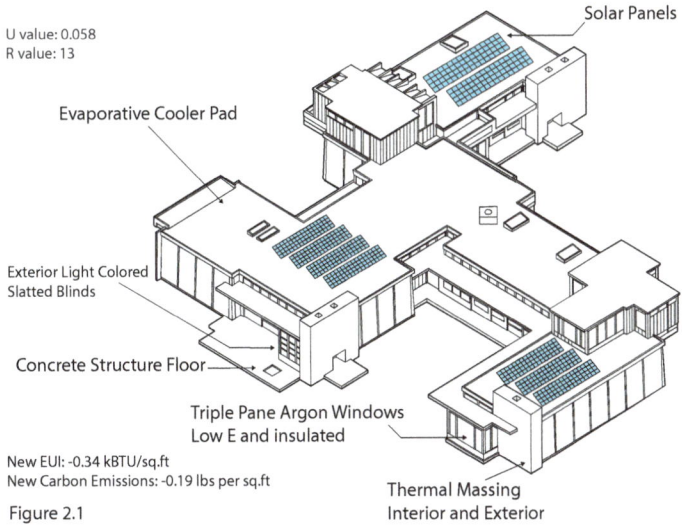

U value: 0.058
R value: 13

- Solar Panels
- Evaporative Cooler Pad
- Exterior Light Colored Slatted Blinds
- Concrete Structure Floor
- Triple Pane Argon Windows Low E and insulated
- Thermal Massing Interior and Exterior

New EUI: -0.34 kBTU/sq.ft
New Carbon Emissions: -0.19 lbs per sq.ft

Figure 2.1

Climate Responsive Strategies

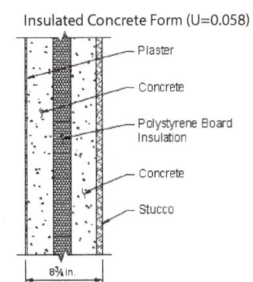

Insulated Concrete Form (U=0.058)
- Plaster
- Concrete
- Polystyrene Board Insulation
- Concrete
- Stucco

8¾ in.

Proposed Wall Section (Figure 2.5)

Existing
- Single Pane 1/8" glass; U=0.89; SHGC=0.64
- Exterior Finish on 8" concrete block; U=0.440

Proposal
- Clear argon triple pane low-E; U=0.22; SHGC=0.21
- Exterior finish on insulated concrete form; U=0.058
- 5kw AC system (Solar panels)
- Exterior light-colored slatted blinds
- Overhang above south facing window
- Evaporative cooler pad
- Large whole house fan
- Concrete structural floor carpeted
- Passive house standard extermely tight air sealing
- Thermal massing
- Electric furnace or baseboards (HSPF = 3.41)

Improved Shade System

6' - 4" Proposed Overhang Projection (OP)
5' Window Height (HP)
38° (VSA)

OP = HP/tan(VSA)
OP = 5/tan(38) = 6.4

Figure 2.2

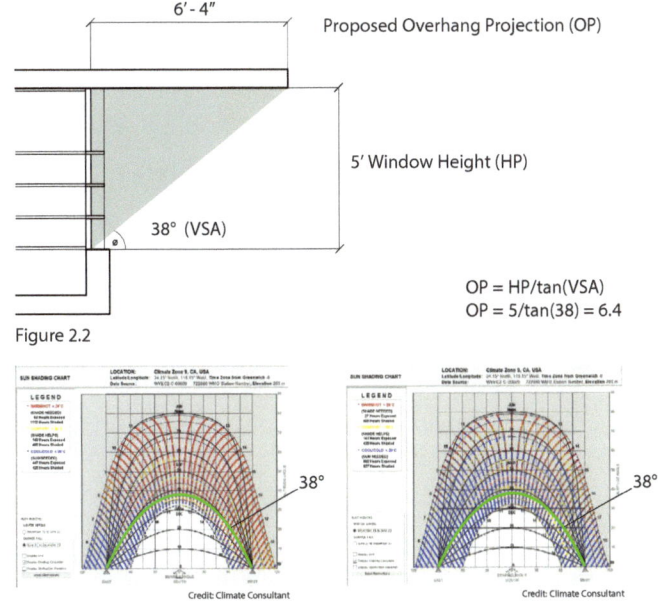

Summer Diagram (Figure 2.3)   Winter Diagram (Figure2.4)

Performance Metrics

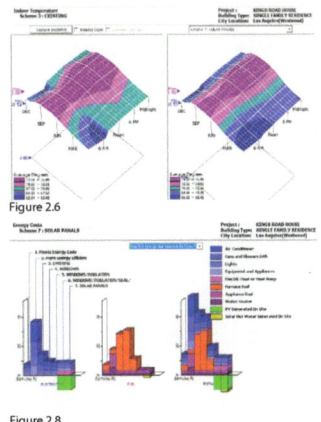

Figure 2.6

Figure 2.7

Figure 2.8

Figure 2.9

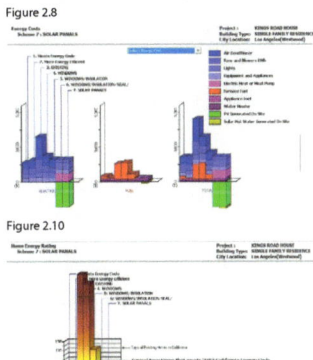

Figure 2.10

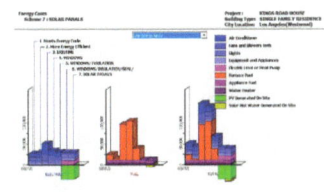

Figure 2.11

Figure 2.12

King's Road House
City, CA | Architect: Rudolf Schindler
Group 18: Mahshid Safarian, Diarra Seck, Adrian Martinez, Rana Matinsefat, Anita Dehmoobad, Haniyeh Poshtareh

Our NZE project featured the Schindler house as a case study located in West Hollywood, CA. This home was nice when we visited it during which offered a cool breeze with the aid of the plant life surrounding. Occupants could also interact with nature through the flat roof sleeping baskets and transparency of glass windows. The current conditions of the home are already energy efficient due to the lack of certain features that newer homes have such as Air conditioning, high efficiency furnace, insulation and so on. The annual energy cost totals to $1,969.93 but despite these factors the house could be more efficient therefore, the team integrated additional scheme proposals that could make the home more up to date with energy codes and operated better in all weather conditions. Scheme 4 switches the single pane windows to double pane and Scheme 5 adds insulation and reflective radiant barriers which were absent in the home. Scheme 6 replaces the floors from concrete to wood which would offer more heat during cooler hours and Scheme7 integrates a heated unit on the 2nd floor, which then prevents heat loss. Scheme 8 was an addition of solar systems in the home which then increased the homes efficiency. The results in The Energy rating predicted that Scheme 4-6-7 seemed to be the top highest on the charts exceeding the (150) mark which weren't working in the buildings favor. Whereas Scheme 5 was the lowest on the chart (130) which worked best following Scheme 8 (140). But the overall combination in Scheme 9 was working because it is (0) which suggests that the combo of the proposals would meet the typical New home that meets 2013 California energy code.

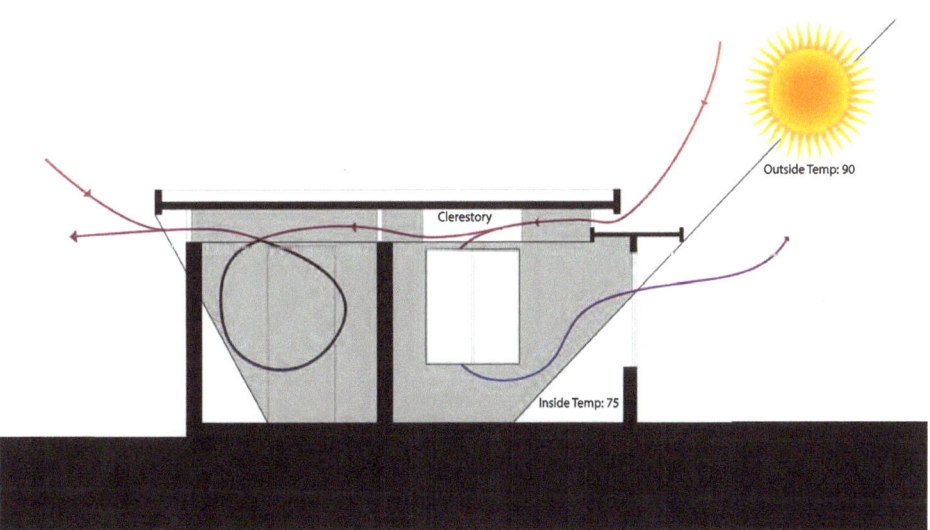

KING'S ROAD

Schindler House

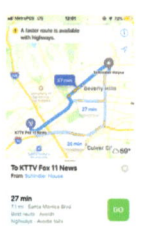

Closest Weather Station to Schindler House

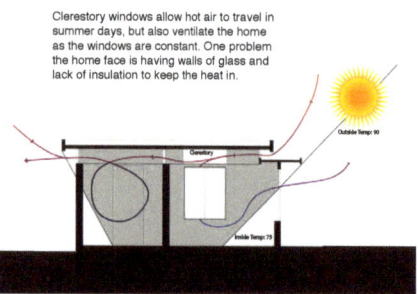

Clerestory windows allow hot air to travel in summer days, but also ventilate the home as the windows are constant. One problem the home face is having walls of glass and lack of insulation to keep the heat in.

2030 PALETTE

Wind Protection

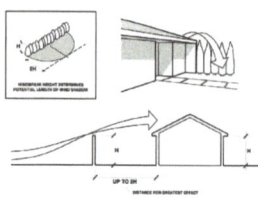

Exterior wind shields or dense planting can protect entries from cold winter winds (wing walls, wind breaks, fences, exterior structures, or land forms)

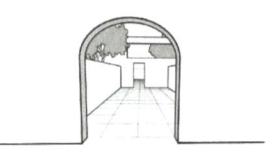

Sunny wind-protected outdoor spaces can extend living areas in cool weather (seasonal sun rooms, enclosed patios, courtyards, or verandahs)

Use Winter Sun

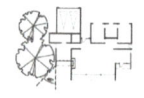

Organize floorplan so winter sun penetrates into daytime use spaces with specific functions that coincide with solar orientation

Use Overhang

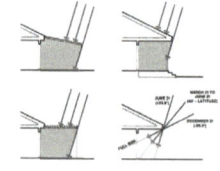

Window overhangs (designed for this latitude) or operable sunshades (awnings that extend in summer) can reduce or eliminate air conditioning

Natural Ventilation

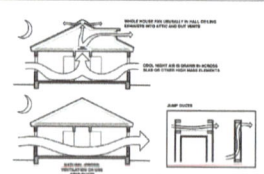

A whole-house fan or natural ventilation can store nighttime 'coolth' in high mass interior surfaces (night flushing), to reduce or eliminate air conditioning

---

This is the Timetable Plot Chart for King Road House (schindler house) from Climate Consultant Application. According to this chart we have the hottest tempetature during May to October usually from 10 am to 6 pm.

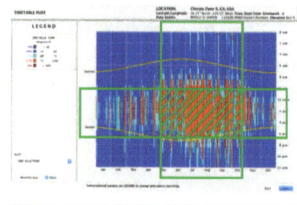

This is Sun Shading Chart For King Road House (Schindler house) from Climate Consultant Application. The Sun Shading Diagram is conducted based on the Timetable Plot Chart (chart above)

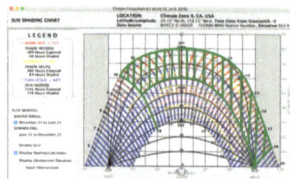

From this elevation of the King Road house we used the building's height and overhang dimension to calculate the vertical shadow angle.

OP = OH / tan VSA
4.5 = 6.9 /tan VSA
VSA = 56 degree

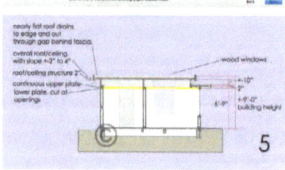

This is temperature chart for King Road House (Schindler House) from Climate Consultant Application. Based on this chart, in this house we can experience the comfort zone in June, July, August, and september.

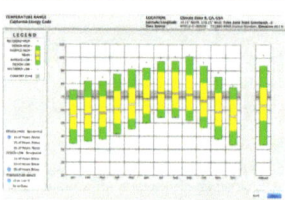

In the Psychrometric chart, by selecting these 5 items, we reached to comfort level of 98% for indoor. These would also save more energy, more money, and environmental friendly.

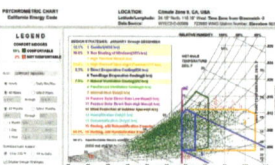

Schindler House

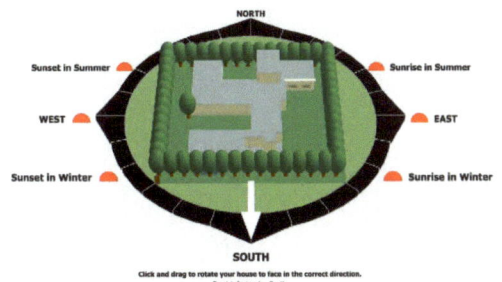

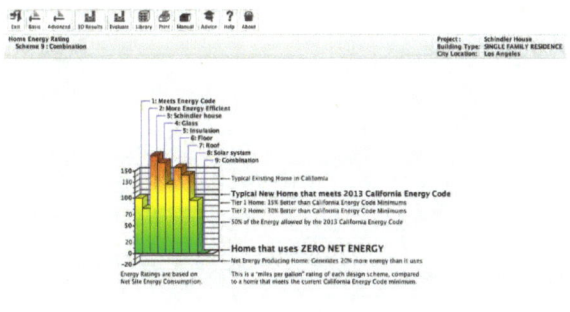

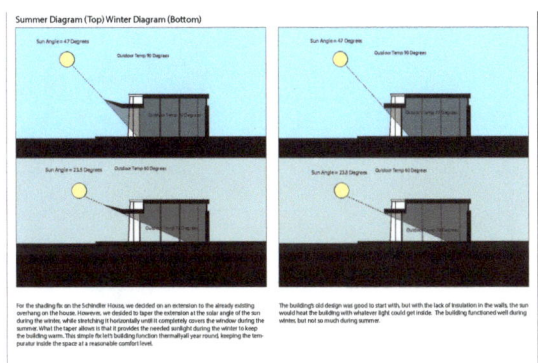

The Annual Energy Cost for Schindler House was $1969.93 yearly, By adding this schemes and 25 solars, we reduced it to $0. The EUI was 179, we reduced that one to 0 as well.

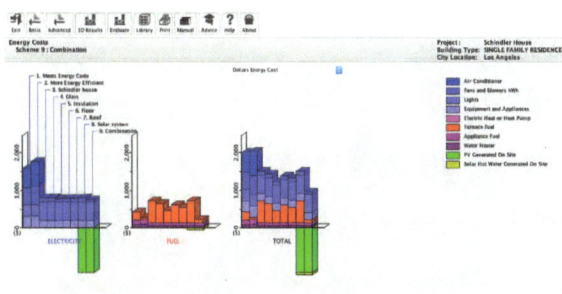

Sustainable Concept Diagram

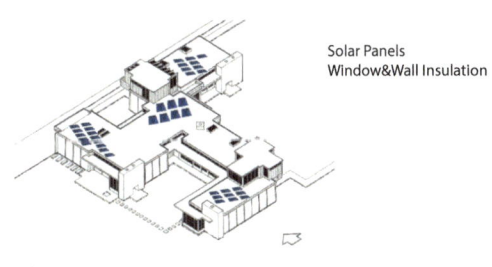

Solar Panels
Window&Wall Insulation

The strategy for sustainability is the use of solar panels and insulation of walls and windows.

U value: 0.058
R value: 13

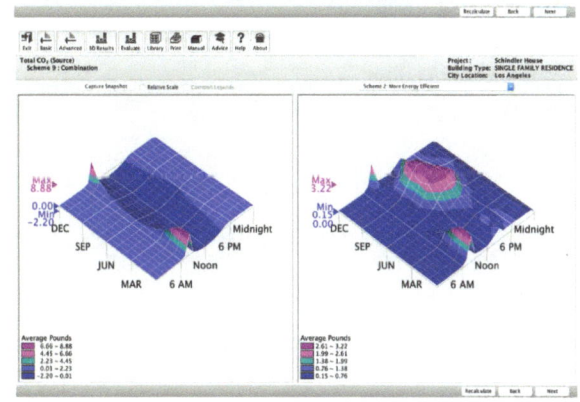

VDL House | City, CA
City, CA | Architect: Richard Neutra

VDL

VDL House | City, CA
City, CA | Architect: Richard Neutra
Group 19: Jose Arce, Cristian Cedillo, Alondra Delgado, Justina Atalla, Alexis Alicea

Proposed Sustainable Strategy

    The existing shading system in the VDL House is an encouragement for passive heating during the winter. Due to the shading system provided by the surrounding environment, the house suffers from relatively high energy expenses during the winter. Thicker thermal mass would be needed in walls, around windows and doors to help preserve inner heat. Also, solar water heating is another option that serves as a passive system for hot and cool water. Additionally, to regulate the temperature of the building and provide ventilation there is the possibility of changing and moving windows to create cross ventilation. The house currently has foil in the interior, which preserves heat, however, it would be encouraged to provide more foil as a design option and as a strategic sustainable way. The original VDL house without passive energy had a total annual energy consumption of 33,057 kwh/year with a total energy cost of around $5,396.13. It also had a EUI (Energy Use Intensity) of around 40.74 kBtu/sqft. This together, the original VDL house has an annual carbon emission of around 17,646.59lbs.

    The current VDL has overhangs that we have extended up to two feet on the east and west on the third floor that will bring more shade into the house. We adjusted the height of the windows to have better ventilation coming inside the house, however, we also have added interior insulation to help preserve the heat for the winter. To reduce the energy consumption of the house we have added 15 solar panels. Our addition of solar panels on the VDL house will successfully have a total annual energy consumption of 7053 kwh/year with a total energy cost of around $1,169.70. The new strategized house will also have a EUI (Energy Use Intensity) of around -1.96 kBtu/sqft.

    Furthermore, our sustainable strategies on the new VDL house has impacted the output of annual carbon emission to -306lbs, causing the residence to be at net zero carbon emission. When searching for an approach to propose sustainable strategies we needed to reach a carbon emission of 0 and below, we added solar and water heating panels. We then continued to change the material of the glass windows, changing them from a clear double pane E in aluminum frame window to a clear argon triple-pane low-E in insulated fiberglass, which has lowered our U-value to 0.22, that is 0.44 lower than the original material in the house. The enhanced insulation has also added two times the R-value of the old model. Lastly, the house's cooling system was changed from air-conditioned to an evaporative cooling system, and that was included along with the other changes that helped us reach a carbon emission of around -306lbs.

15 Solar Panels: tilt - 36.78 degrees
Solar Water Heating
Evaporative Cooling
Cross Ventilation
Night Vent Cooling
EUI: -1.96 kBtu

Windows are clear argon triple pane low-E in insulated fiberglass.
SHGC: 0.21
U-value: 0.22
VLT: 0.44

VDL

VDL HOUSE
by Neutra

CLIMATE ANALYSIS
The Neutra VDL house located in Los Angeles of Climate Zone 9. It is 8.88 miles apart from the nearest National Weather Service.

The US National Weather Service corresponds to the Bob Hope Airport. The service reports various resources other than flight services such as predictions, locations and data/records.

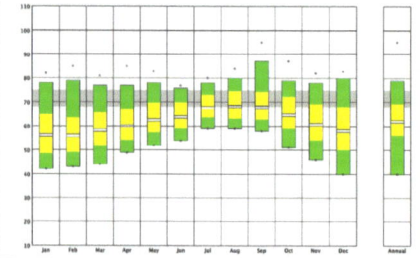

The Temperature Range chart shows that for the months from June through September, the comfort zone is reached. For the rest of the months, the temperature is below the comfort zone level.

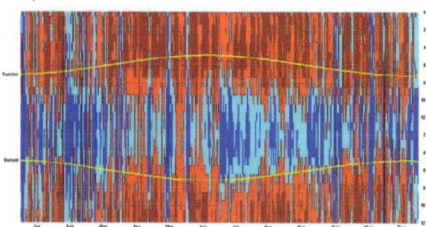

EXISTING SHADE

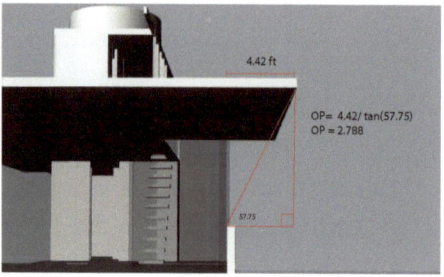

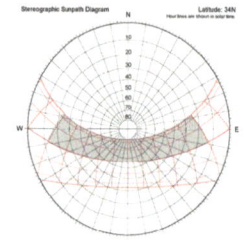

RESPONSIVE DESIGN

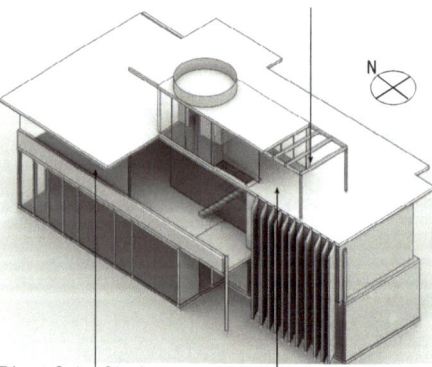

Direct Gain: Glazing   Night Vent Cooling
EUI: 40.74 kBtu

Windows are clear double pane E in aluminum frame.
SHGC: 0.40
U-value: 0.66
VLT: 0.63

R-value for walls: 15.38

BIOCLIMATIC STRATEGIES

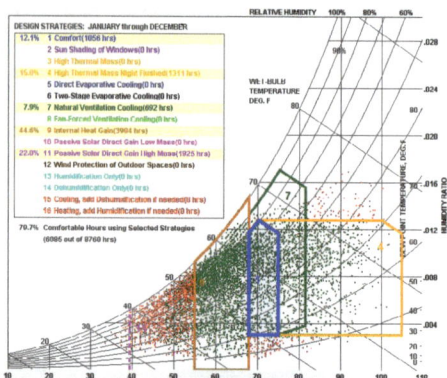

Direct Gain: Glazing
Solar glazing provides passive heating in the winter by directing sunlight into spaces.

Night Vent Cooling
Thermal mass cooled at night, absorbs heat and provides cooled indoor spaces and surfaces. Thermal mass can be incorporated into walls, floors, and ceilings.

Cross Ventilation
Take advantage of natural wind currents to cool/ventillate building. Locate window openings perpendicular to winds and add opening on opposite side of space.
Source: ARC2030 Palette

VDL HOUSE
by Neutra

PROPOSED STRATEGIES

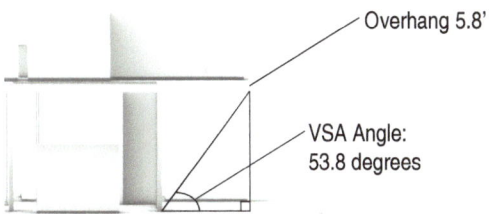

The VSA angle was calculated based on the location set at noon on May 1st and the result was 53.8 degrees. The necessary overhang for the 8 ft window facing east was calculated to be 5.8 ft.

Cross Ventilation, Triple Pane Windows, Night Vent Cooling, Solar Water Heating, & Evaporative Cooling

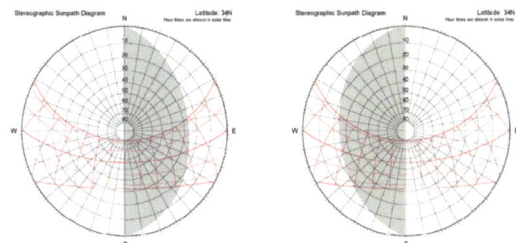

- Passive cooling through natural air movement
- Better insulation and temperature regulation

- Providing cool indoor surfaces during the day and flushing heat from the space

- solar radiation captured offsetting fossil fuel combustion

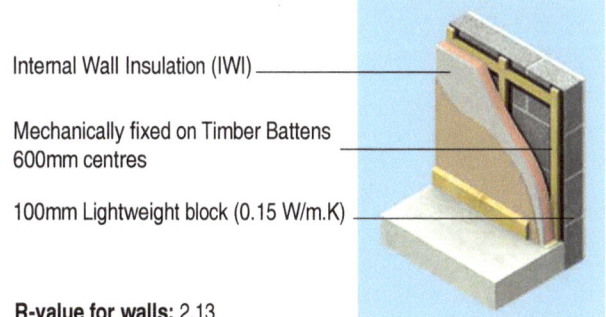

- Internal Wall Insulation (IWI)
- Mechanically fixed on Timber Battens 600mm centres
- 100mm Lightweight block (0.15 W/m.K)

R-value for walls: 2.13

PERFORMANCE METRICS

	Original VDL house (w/out passive energy)	VDL house (w/ passive energy)
Total Annual Energy Consumption	33057 kWh/year	7053 kWh/year
Total Annual Energy cost (dollars)	$5,396.13	$1,169.70
Energy Use Intensity (EUI)	40.74 kBtu/sqf	-1.96 kBtu/sqf
Annual Carbon Emission (lbs)	17,646.59 lbs.	-306 lbs.

VDL House without Passive Energy: South Facing Window

VDL House without Passive Energy: South Facing Window

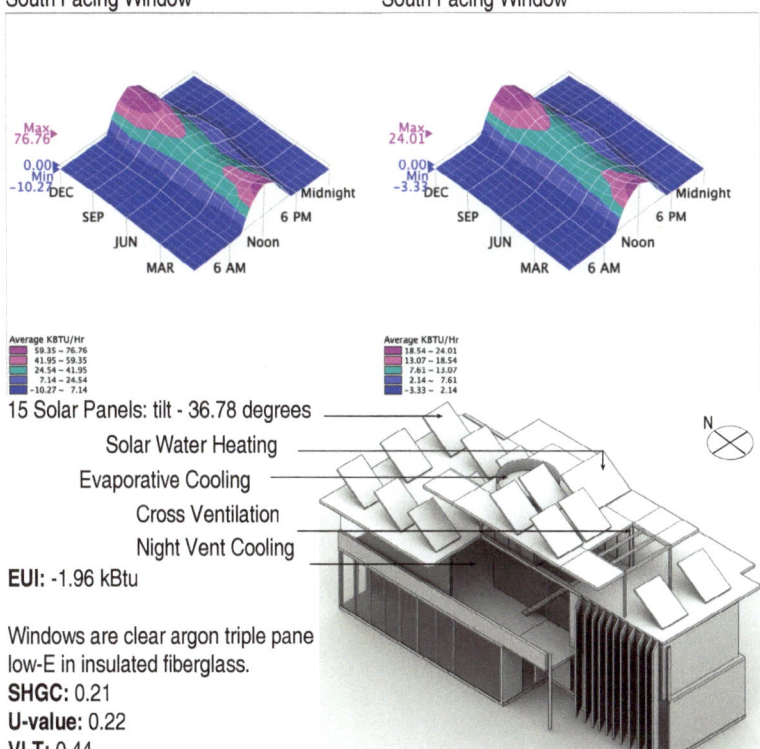

15 Solar Panels: tilt - 36.78 degrees
Solar Water Heating
Evaporative Cooling
Cross Ventilation
Night Vent Cooling

EUI: -1.96 kBtu

Windows are clear argon triple pane low-E in insulated fiberglass.
SHGC: 0.21
U-value: 0.22
VLT: 0.44

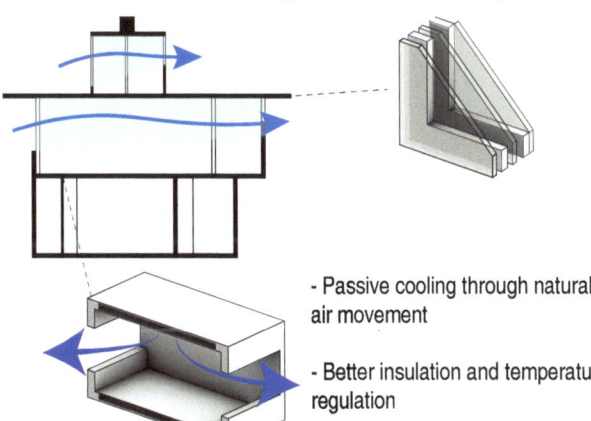

VDL House | City, CA
City, CA | Architect: Richard Neutra
Group 20: Khanh Dinh, Toan Nguyen, Eduardo De La Rosa, Huda Alhassan, George Jang

We are working to improve the current existing conditions of the VDL House to make it NZE (net zero energy) building. The original VDL House was built pre 1978 with the building standards and materials available pre 1978 it is assumed that the EUI (energy use intensity) of the building itself is very high consuming 30 kBTU/sq ft of fuel and electricity and producing 20,000 lbs of CO_2. By adding some simple upgrades to the current conditions, we are trying to achieve a better performance out of the building. The better performance is measure by a decrease consumption of energy to the point of zero. The three strategies proposed are adding or upgrading the insulation, replacing and upgrading all windows with ones with lower u-values, and enhancing the some of the old features with modern technology. The first improvement adding insulation, "Super Insulation to 2.0 times the current code R- Values, by doing this this will allow people to better control the internal environment and maintain comfortability. Another strategy in mind was to upgrade the current windows to a "Clear Double Pane Low-E in Insulated Fiberglass/Vinyl frame" or "Clear Argon Triple Pane Low-E in Insulated Fiberglass/Vinyl frame" type. By doing this we will lower our u-value of the windows to .32-.22 which means there will be less heat transferred through conductance and infiltration in the building better maintaining the internal comfortability. In the VDL House natural ventilation was a key part of the original design of the building and propose to maintain this feature. We propose to update the design my adding an "Indoor Air Velocity for Cooling" system to force air through when the temperature between the exterior and the interior are the same to create air movement. By doing this the air motion will be increased to 300 FPM which will feel effectively 6.6F degrees cooler in a space.

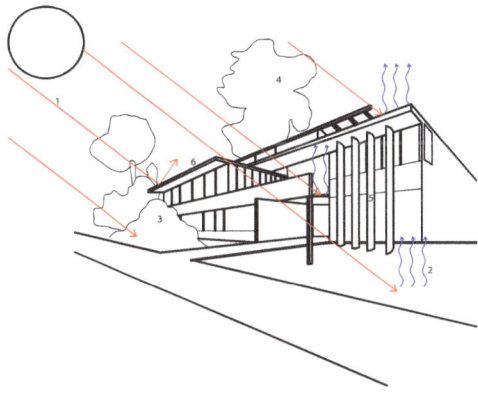

VDL

NZE PROJECT
CLIMATE & BUILDING ANALYSIS

VDL HOUSE

Group 14: Khanh Dinh, Toan Nguyen, Eduardo De La Rosa, Huda Alhassan, George Jang

CLIMATE ZONE

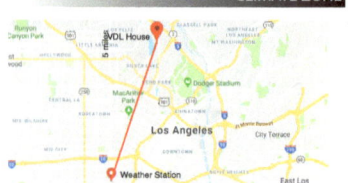

1 California Climate Zone 9

Location:
Address: 2300 Silver Lake Boulevard
City: Los Angeles, CA 90039
Coordinates: Latitude: 34.098468 | Longitude: -118.260522

Climate Zone Description:
A Southern California inland valley climate influence by coastal and inland weather. The localized effect of the Santa Ana winds bring warm dry air into the area and the Pacific coast pushes in marine air that is cool and moist.

Distance from Case Study to Weather Station: 5

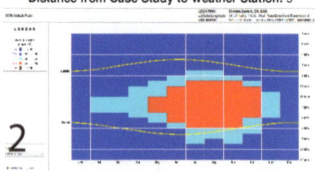

2

Monthly Temperature Range:
Temperatures between 75°F and 100°F occur the longest period of time durning the months of July and September.
Between 9am to 6pm.

Temperatures between 75°F and 100°F also occur during the months of May, June and October.
Between 10am to 5pm.

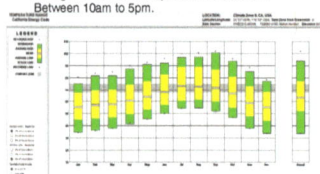

Average Temperature Range:
The annual average temperature range in California Climate Zone 9 is between 55°F and 75°F. The Average temperature is 65°F which sits 10°F below the comfort zone.

Temperature Maximums and Minimum Range:
During the summer months May though October Extreme Maximum Temperatures range between 95°F and 105°F. Over the winter months, November through February Extreme Minimum Temperatures range between 34°F and 40°F.

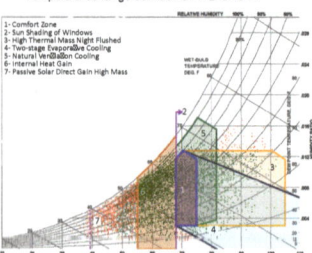
1- Comfort Zone
2- Sun Shading of Windows
3- High Thermal Mass Night Flushed
4- Two-stage Evaporative Cooling
5- Natural Ventilation
6- Internal Heat Gain
7- Passive Solar Direct Gain High Mass

OVERHEATED & UNDERHEATED PERIODS

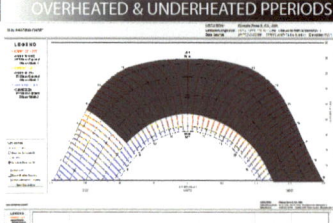

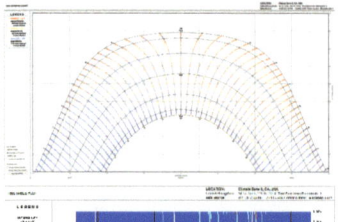

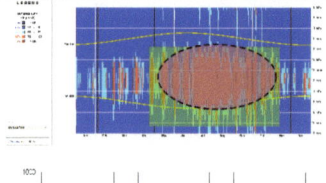

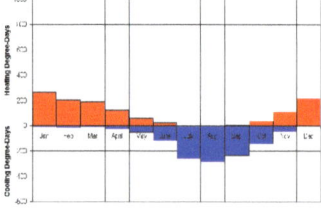

According to the chart it a warming trend begins in the month of May and lasts until October. The Timetable plot shows that in the summer months the heating period starts at 8am to 7pm. However, during the rest of the year 63% of the time temperatures ranges between 32°F to 68°F

EXISTING SHADE

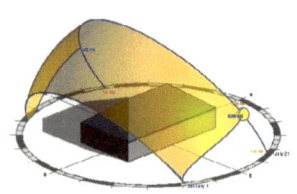

RESPONSE TO CLIMATE

Window-Glazing	Clear Argon Double Pan Low-E in aluminum frame (U=0.09 SHGC=0.5)
Exterior Walls	Stucco, Vinyl or Wood, 1"+Polystyrene, Plywood, 2x4 Wood Stud @16" O.C., PLaster board (R=41, U=0.024)
Floors	Slab on Grade covered by carpet or casework
Roof	Default Flat or low Sloped Roof (U=0.031)
Ventilation and Infiltration	High natural ventilation can add up to 20. air change if needed
HVAC System	Best Available Furnace, Condensation Furnace (98% AFUE)
Insulation	Wall R=13, Ceiling R=30, Floor R=0

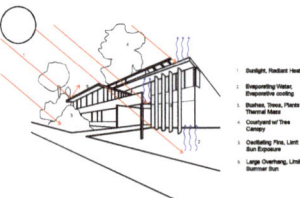

- Sunlight, Radiant Heat
- Evaporating Water, Evaporative cooling
- Bushes, Trees, Plants
- Courtyard w/ Tree Canopy
- Osciallating Fins, Limit Sun Exposure
- Large Overhang, Limit Summer Sun

BIOCLIMATIC STRATEGIES

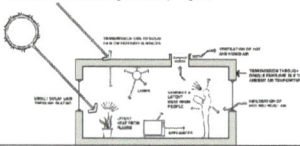
Figue 1.1

Figue 2.1

Strategy 1
External shading devices can reduce solar heat gain through glazing by up to 80%. By designing shading devices according to the sun's seasonal path, both summer shading and winter solar gain can be achieved in climates with seasonal variations.

The VDL House is in the northern hemisphere with south facing windows incorporating horizontal overhangs or louvers for those windows will provide shading during the overheating months throughout the year. Some currently existing examples include "The Leo and Dottie Kolligian Library" fig 1.1

Strategy 2
High mass interior surfaces (tile, slate, stone, brick or adobe) feel naturally cool on hot days and can reduce day-to-night temperature swings

In California Climate Zone 9 Thermal mass is a great way to cool a space during the day and heat a space during the night. Since the climate in zone 9 is warm and dry during most of the year and diurnal temperature changes of 20 F or more a met, incorporating thermal mass walls will help reduce the use of off-site energy sources to maintain a comfortable space. An example of this is Germantown Friends School by SMP Architects fig 2.1.

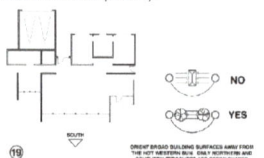

Heat Gains
Heat gain from lights, people, and equipment greatly reduces heating needs so keep home tight, well insulated (to lower Balance Point temperature).

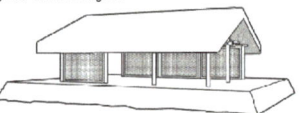

Passive Homes
Traditional passive homes in temperate climates used light weight construction with slab on grade and operable walls and shaded outdoor spaces.

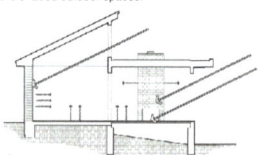

Passive Solar Heating and Shading
For passive solar heating face most of the glass area south to maximize winter sun exposure, but design overhangs to fully shade in summer.

High Thermal Mass
Use high mass interior surfaces like slab floors, high mass walls, and a stone fireplace to store winter passive heat and summer night 'coolth'.

VDL

DESIGN PROPOSAL

PERFORMANCE METRICS

Existing

Site Energy Consumption	17.21 kWh/sqft
Total Annual Energy Cost	$9925.17
Energy Use Intensity	58.71 kBUT/sqft
Carbon Emmisions	9.06 lbs/sqft

Proposed

Site Energy Consumption	4.84 kWh/sqft
Total Annual Energy Cost	$1,622.43
Energy Use Intensity	16.5 kBUT/sqft
Carbon Emmisions	2.99 lbs/sqft

PERFORMANCE METRICS

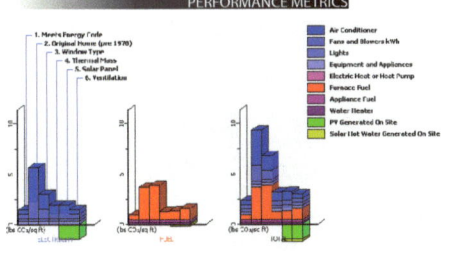

CO2 Production

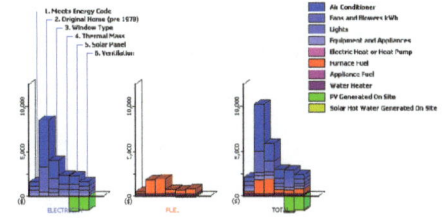

New Energy Cost

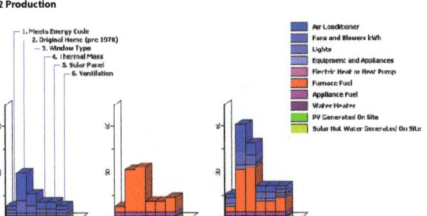

EUI (Energy Usage Intensity)

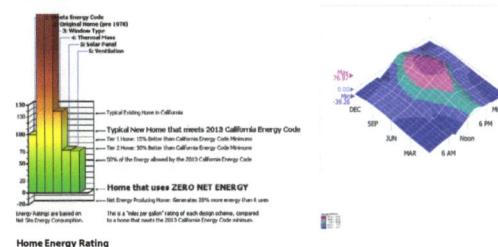

Home Energy Rating

RESPONSE TO CLIMATE STRATEGIES and SUSTAINABLE CONCEPT DIAGRAMS

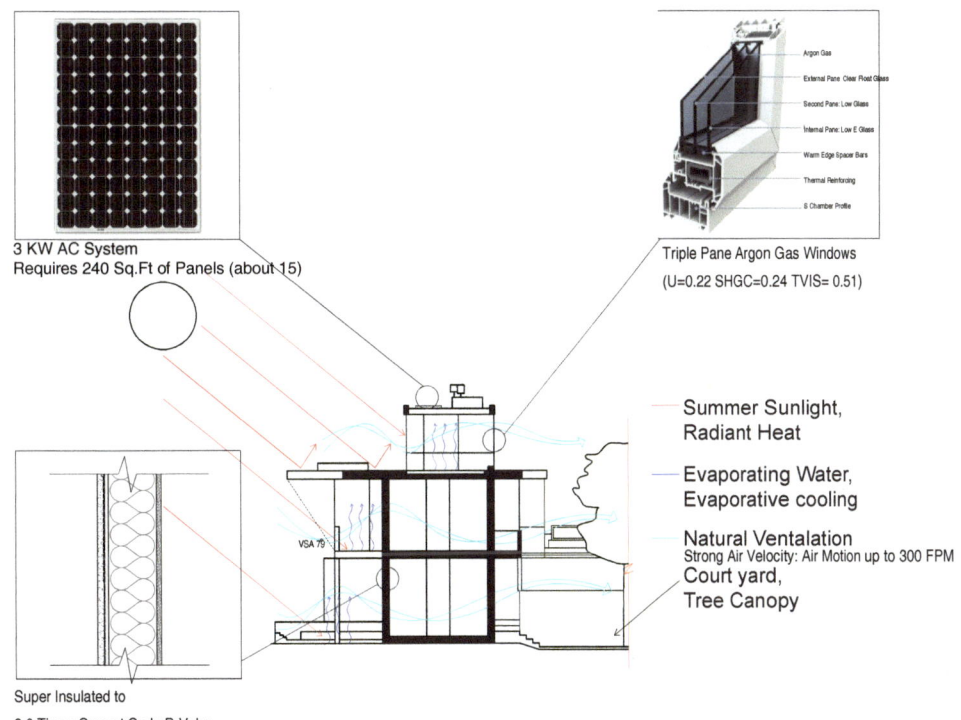

3 KW AC System
Requires 240 Sq.Ft of Panels (about 15)

Triple Pane Argon Gas Windows
(U=0.22 SHGC=0.24 TVIS= 0.51)

Super Insulated to
2.0 Times Current Code R-Value

— Summer Sunlight, Radiant Heat

— Evaporating Water, Evaporative cooling

— Natural Ventalation
Strong Air Velocity: Air Motion up to 300 FPM
Court yard,
Tree Canopy

VDL House | City, CA
City, CA | Architect: Richard Neutra
Group 21: Noel Cordero, Ulysses Ojeda, Gabriella Torres, Cho Zin Theint, Daniela Varg

The existing VDL house has a clear Single Pane 1/8" Glass in Aluminum Frame, No Insulation as it was built before 1978, the exterior finish on 2"x6" wood studs, it is an early energy code building, low efficiency furnace and air conditioner, and no solar PV and solar water heating. Even though this building was seemingly sustainable, it has plenty of issues with sustainability when it gets put into the world we have today where technology is extremely advanced and a great portion of things have changed since it was built. The conditions we proposed for this building would be changing the original windows to the clear argon triple pane Low-E insulated Fiberglass/Vinyl Frame, adding super insulation for the building, creating an exterior finish on +1" Rigid Foam Board on 2"x6" wood studs, upgrading it to a passive house standard, changing to an electric furnace, and adding 15 panels of solar water heating system. Adding and upgrading these proposed sustainable strategies would help this building reach net zero energy. In changing the window it decreases the U Value, SHGC, and the VLT for the house. Adding super insulation would make this building be warm in the winter without having to use other methods that are not as sustainable. Changing from the low efficiency furnace and air conditioner to the electric furnace or baseboards and evaporative cooler would make this building use less energy and still get a better heating system. The Solar panels would generate the energy that the building would be needing, so that it uses less of the outside resources.

Vertical Sun Angle

VSA = tan^-1(5.01ft/5ft)
VSA = 44.92 degrees

VDL

Current Climate

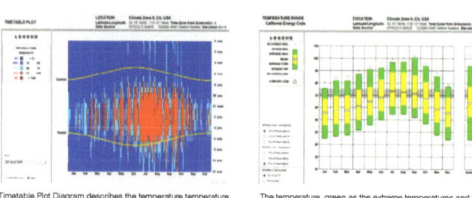

Timetable Plot Diagram describes the temperature temperature throughout the different times of the day.

The temperature, green as the extreme temperatures and the yellow as the median temperatures within the climate zone.

Sun Shading Chart describes where the sun during a certain time of day during certain months. The red indicates the time the weather is hot and the blue indicates the cooling period.

California Climate Zone: 9

Location: 2300 Silver Lake Blvd
Los Angeles, CA 90039

Data Source: WYEC2-C-00009
722880 WMO Station Number

Elevation: 863 ft

Closest Weather Station: 5 minutes;
1.2 Miles

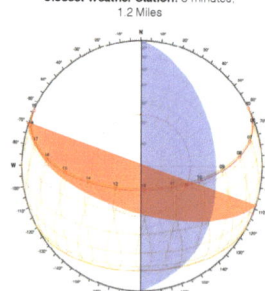

Weather File Location

Bob Hope Airport, 2627 N Hollywood Way, Burbank, CA 91505, 8.85 miles away from the VDL House

Psychrometric Chart indicating the comfort zone and how the design strategies are going to affect the comfort zones, and type of strategies will help improve the comfort zone.

Verticle Sun Angle

VSA = tan^-1(5.01ft/5ft)
VSA = 44.92 degrees

Existing Conditions

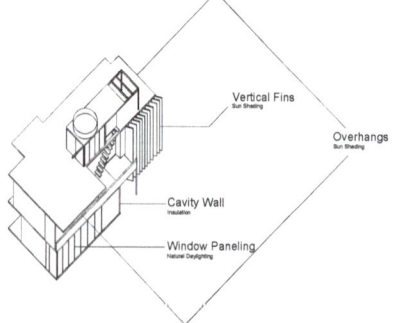

- Vertical Fins — Sun Shading
- Overhangs — Sun Shading
- Cavity Wall — Insulation
- Window Paneling — Natural Daylighting

2030 Palette

Sun Shading of Windows 20.8%

Passive Solar Direct Gain High Mass 22%

Internal Heat Gain 44.6%

High Thermal Mass Night Flushed 15%

Heating, add Humidification if Needed 17.6%

Window Type:
Single Glazing
U-Factor: 1.25
SHGC: 0.76
VT: 0.74

Double Glazing
U-Factor: 0.32
SHGC: 0.3
VT: 0.5

The main sustainable design in this house would be the terrace and its natural ventilation system which flows along the house. The green space makes this building sustainable because this leads nature into the house. The vertical fins that were added outside the house as a shading device. The trees in front of the house are also used as a shading device so that during summer the sunlight can be blocked while during winter the sunlight can be brought into the building while the trees wither. The overhangs are used to block the sunlight from getting into the house directly at an angle, which makes this sustainable for this building.

Bioclimatic Strategies
Recommended Strategies:

- Sun Shading of windows 20.8%

- High Thermal Mass Night Flushed 15%

- Natural Ventilation Cooling 7.9%

- Internal Heat Gain 44.6%

- Passive Solar Direct Gain High Mass 22%

- Heating, add Humidification if Needed 17.6%

Group 19: Noel Cordero, Ulysses Ojeda, Cho Zin Theint, Gabriella Torres, Daniela Vargas

Implementation of Strategies to Reach Net Zero Energy

Proposed Improvements and Energy Costs

Design Strategies	Net Energy (kWh)
Existing House	44,330
Windows	34,332
Insulation	32,321
Wall Assembly	13,285
Infiltration System	11,013
Heating and Cooling	6,970
Solar Systems	-578

Energy Use Intensity

EUI	Btu/sqft
Existing House	65
Windows	49
Insulation	48
Wall Assembly	19
Infiltration System	16
Heating and Cooling	10
Solar Systems	-1

Annual Carbon Emissions

	Total (lbs per sqft)
Existing House	9.93
Windows	7.17
Insulation	6.89
Wall Assembly	3.10
Infiltration System	2.77
Heating and Cooling	1.63
Solar Systems	-0.36

NET ENERGY

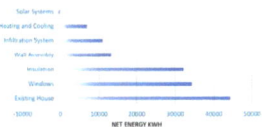

ENERGY USE INTENSITY

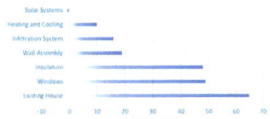

ANNUAL CARBON EMISSIONS

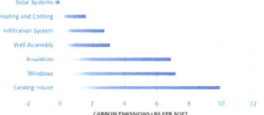

New Implemented Strategies

Windows
We replaced our single pane 1/8" window with clear argon triple pane low-E windows in fiber glass frames. Better window insulation reduces 40,680 kWh per year. Triple paned windows helps reduce the amount of sun rays actually entering the building.

Clear Argon Triple Pane Low - E in Insulated Fiberglass/Vinyl Frame

Wall Assembly
The VDL House's walls were improved. Structurally they remained the same as the existing homes, with 2" x 6" wood studs every 24." Now the VDL's walls are set with cavity insulation.

Heating and Cooling
We replaced the low efficiency furnace and air conditioner with an electric furnace and an evaporative cooler with pad efficiency of 85% which completely eliminates the need for any other air conditioner system. The improved heating and cooling systems, represent, an estimated yearly reduction of about $7,000 in enery costs.

Exterior Finish on +1" Rigid Foam Board on 2" x 4" Wood Studs with R21 Cavity Insulation

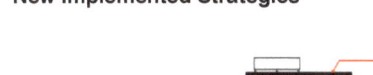

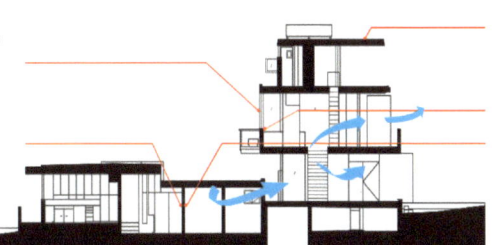

Solar Systems
In applying 15 Photovoltic Panels, an estimated 7,488 kWh of clean energy is generated per year, which saves approximately $1,744.50 annually and reduces CO2 emmissions that would have been produced from non-renewable fuels.

Infiltration
Extremely tight air sealing minimizes the amount of hot and cool air entering the building's envelop. This reduces the probablity of the building's interior temperate and space conditions from being affected from the exterior.

Insulation
We improved the existing VL House's uninsulated walls with Super insulation which, like the current infiltrations system we are placing, will work to keep the interior of the building free of the climatic conditions of the houses' exterior.

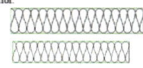

3kW AC System - 15 Panels and Solar Water Heating System

Passive House Standard; Extremely Tight Air Sealing

Super Insulation to 2.0 Times Current Code R-Values

Existing VDL House

Clear Single Pane 1/8" Glass in Aluminum Frame
U Value: 0.89
SHGC: 0.64
VLT: 0.66

No Insulation: Vintage House built before 1978
Wall R: 0
Ceiling R: 0
Floor R: 0

Exterior finish on 2" x 6" Wood Studs with no Cavity Insulation
U Value: 0.359

Early Energy Code Building
SLA: 4.9
9.8 ACH 50: 9.8

Older Low Efficiency Furnace and Air Conditioner
Cooling System; SEER: 8.9
Heating System; AFUE: 72%

No Solar PV and Solar Water Heating
Sq. ft: NA

HEED Diagram with Proposed Strategies

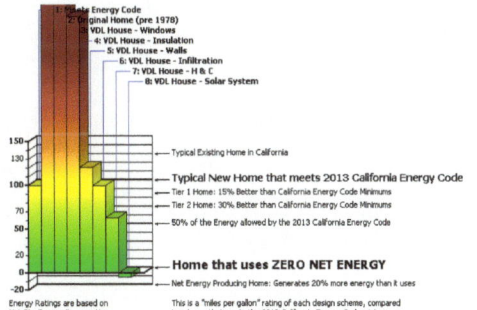

Proposed Conditions

Clear Argon Triple Pane Low - E in Insulated Fiberglass/Vinyl Frame
U Value: 0.22
SHGC: 0.21
VLT: 0.44

Super Insulation to 2.0 Times Current Code R-Values
2.0 times Current Code R-Values

Exterior Finish on +1" Rigid Foam Board on 2" x 6" Wood Studs with R21 Cavity Insulation
U Value: 0.065

Passive House Standard; Extremely Tight Air Sealing
SLA: 0.3
9.8 ACH 50: 0.6

Electric Furnace or Baseboards and Evaporative Cooler
Pad Efficiency: 85%
Heating System; HSPF: 3.41

3 kW AC System - 15 Panels and Solar Water Heating System
Sq. ft: 240

Group 19: Noel Cordero, Ulysses Ojeda, Cho Zin Theint, Gabriella Torres, Daniela Vargas

VDL House | City, CA
City, CA | Architect: Richard Neutra
Group 22: Enrique Mora, Jorge Torres, Robert Ambriz, Alex Tapia, Cynthia Martinez

In order to make the VDL house more sustainable we began by adding a 4kw AC system with 20 solar panels. These solar panels will generate electricity for the house, allowing the house to rely less on drawing electricity from the grid and lower electricity costs for the building. We also added a solar water heating system which does not utilize gas and is 100% efficient as it runs on electricity generated by the solar panels, further lowering electricity costs and dependability on the grid to provide electricity. We removed any fan forced ventilation as the large amount of windows and openings in the building, as well as the large amount of shading and comfortable California climate, allow for adequate natural ventilation to ensure proper ventilation of the whole household. This also saves on electricity costs and there are no constantly moving fans to suck electricity from the house. We extended an overhang on the second floor over the front balcony opening in order to provide better shading to the inside room as well as the outer balcony. This shading will help to cool off the inside room. We kept the fixed overhangs as the climate in California tends to stay sunny all year long and there is no reason need to optimize the shading in order to optimize heat gain for winter. We reduced infiltration into the house by upgrading the sealing to the Passive House Standard with extremely tight air sealing. This allows for less hot air to enter the house as well as less cold air to be lost. It also increased the quality of the air inside the building along with the constantly running ventilation fan that is required in California homes in order to provide fresh air. We changed the frames of the windows from aluminum to vinyl and fiberglass in order to prevent heat from being conducted through the metal into the house. We also replaced the thin single and double pane windows to clear argon triple pane low-E windows. These windows will drastically reduce heath infiltration into the house while still allowing a large amount of light in due to the fact that the building has a large amount of windows which were a major source of heat gain with the thinner windows. Along with this we upgraded the buildings insulation to super insulation that is 2 times the current code R-values for California homes. This, along with rigid foam board and cavity insulation in the walls, further prevents heat gain within the building, allowing for the building to cool and remain cool more efficiently. We also added a radiant barrier in the attic to further prevent heat gain by reflecting heat and preventing heat gain through radiance. All of these modifications to the building allow for the building to achieve a -20 energy code rating, well below the zero net energy qualification of 0. This is down from the original rating of well above 150, surpassing modern energy codes by nearly 2 times.

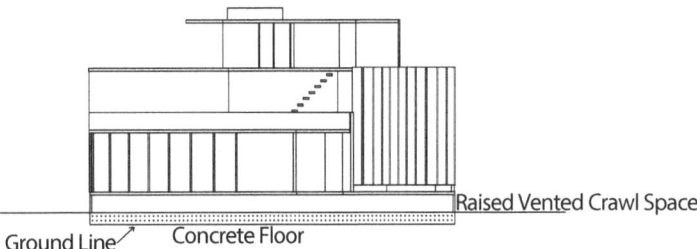

VDL

NEUTRA VDL HOUSE
CLIMATE and BUILDING ANALYSIS

GROUP 22 MEMBERS
ROBERT AMBRIZ, ALEX TAPIA, CYNTHIA MARTINEZ, ENRIQUE MORA, JORGE TORRES

CLIMATE ZONE

1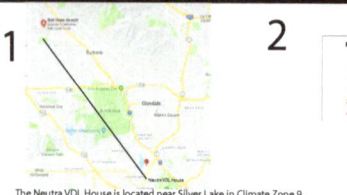
The Neutra VDL House is located near Silver Lake in Climate Zone 9. The Weather Data locator is approximately 9.10 miles away at the Bob Hope Airport.

2
For most of the year, the relative humidity is arond 60%, except for the months through January-March, and October-December where it drops between 2%-20%.

3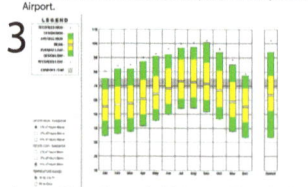
For most of the months except for July, August, and September, the avergae temperature is below the comfort zone.

4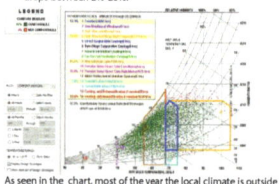
As seen in the chart, most of the year the local climate is outside the comfort zone(the box in blue).

EXISTING SHADE

1

4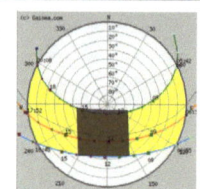
VSA on Sun

3 Area Shaded with HSA
Based on the analysis used, we were able to plot the area which needs the sun shading projection on the vertical solar path diagram.

Based on the diagrams(Vertical Solar Path, Shadow Angles Projector, and the Shadow Angle of the Shading Element), we were able to identify which parts needed to be shaded.

OVERHEATED and UNDERHEATED PERIODS

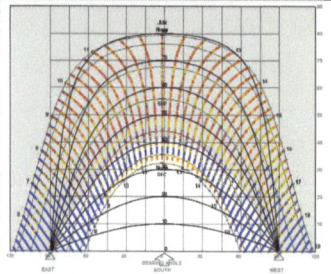
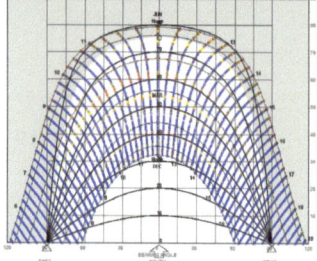

LEGEND
- WARM/HOT > 78°F
  (SHADE NEEDED)
  43 Hours Exposed
  43 Hours Shaded
- COMFORT - 68°F
  (SHADE HELPS)
  187 Hours Exposed
  239 Hours Shaded
- COOL/COLD < 68°F
  (SUN NEEDED)
  1320 Hours Exposed
  697 Hours Shaded

1 Sun Shade Needed
JUNE 21 - DEC 21
June- 10 am - 5 pm
July- 6 am - 6 pm
August- 7:30 am - 4 pm
September- 9 am - 4 pm

Sun Light Needed
October- 6 am- 4 pm
November- 6 am - 6 pm
December- 6 am - 6 pm

2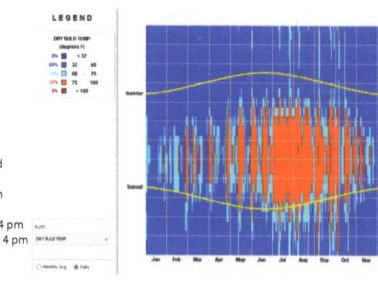
Sun Light Needed
DEC 21 - JUNE 21
December- 6 am - 6 pm
January- 6 am - 6 pm
February - 6 am - 5pm
March- 6am - 5 pm
April- 7 am - 5 pm
May- 6 am- 5 pm

Sun Shade Needed
June- 10 am - 5 pm

RESPONSE TO CLIMATE

1 The Neutra VDL II house is primarily made sustainable due to its excellent shading systems and in how it allows an abundance on natural light inside when needed.

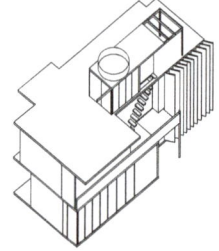

The fins (red) on the front facade shade from northern sunlight while the overhangs (blue) throughout the house shade from southern sunlight.

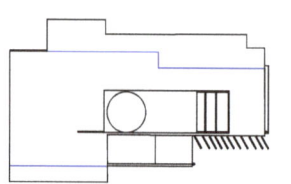

2 A key feature of how the Neutra VDL II house is able to regulate the amount of sunlight which enters the building are the operable fins on the front facade of the house.

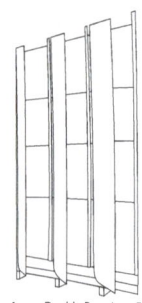

3 Windows: Clear Argon Double Pane Low-E in aluminum frame
Walls: Stucco, Polystyrene, Plywood, and Plaster Board

SHGC: The amount of solar radiation which is absorbed by windows and subsequently released inward.
SHGC = 0.5

U Value: The heat transmission through a part of a building.
U Value (of windows): 0.69 , U Value (of walls): 0.024 , U Value (of roof): 0.031

VLT: Visible Light Transmittance; amount of visible light which passes through a window.
VLT: 0.6

R Value: The capacity of an insulating material to resist the flow of heat.
R Value (of exterior walls): 41

BIOCLIMATIC STRATEGIES

High Thermal Mass Night Flushed
One strategy that can be used to achieve thermal comfort would be by trying to use the cool night wind to your advantage. The use of the cool night wind as ventilation is a great option, especially as how the VDL House actually has some of that. There is an open staircase that can allow ventilation to both the third and second floor. There are also glass walls that open onto the patio gardens. Having more of this design around the house will allow for better ventilation without the use of artificial sources.

On the right, you can see the open staircase over the balcony.

Internal Heat Gain
Another strategy that can be used to achieve thermal comfort could be by regulating the heat transfer in the house. The use of hallways (made of wood) leading into certain rooms is a perfect way of controlling heat transfer as it controls the movement of people, which aside from outside sources, provide the most heat and affect the relative humidity.

On the right, you can see a hallway that spans almost the entire lenth of the house.

Passive Solar Direct Gain Heat Mass
One last strategy that can be used to achieve thermal comfort could be with how certain materials absorb and maintain heat. The use of this strategy requires that the south-side facing wall of the house have windows to be able to bring solar energy directly into the house, which will allow certain materials to absorb that energy and re-radiate it back into the room, warming it up. In the house, all sides have windows/glass except for the south facing side of the house.

On the left, you can see the soth facing wall. Most of its covered by wood. Adding windows/glass would definitely allow rooms to warm up faster.

120

NEUTRA VDL HOUSE
DESIGN PROPOSAL
PROPOSED CLIMATE RESPONSIVE STRATEGIES

As of 2003, homes in Califronia were required to have an Energy Rating of 100 . The VDL House however was re-built with the pre -1978 Energy code, making the Rating of the house much higher at 387.

- Home Meeting Energy Code
- Neutra House at 1978
- Proposal 1
- Proposal 2
- Proposal 3
- Proposal 4
- Proposal 5

The VDL wasn't built with strict Energy Codes in mind, meaning it was highly inefficient. The following proposals are aimed at reducing the energy consumption of the building until it becomes a much more efficient net zero building.

PROPOSAL 3

Our third proposal included replacing the floor with cooncrete and adding a raised vented crawl space in order to help cool the space and allow more air flow. This reduced the rating from163 to 104.

PROPOSAL 1 & 2

Our first proposal included switching out the aluminum window frames for wood, vinyl or fiberglass frames as to prevent heat loss/gain through conduction. This reduced the energy rating from 387 to 233.

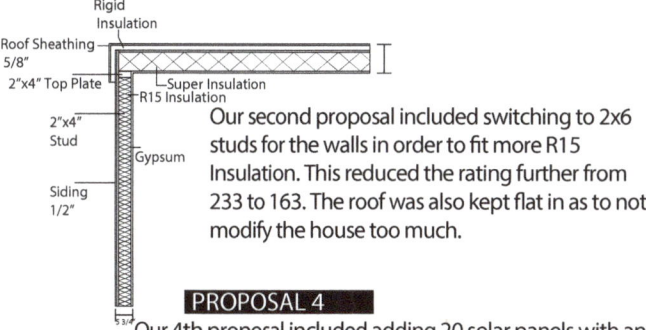

Our second proposal included switching to 2x6 studs for the walls in order to fit more R15 Insulation. This reduced the rating further from 233 to 163. The roof was also kept flat in as to not modify the house too much.

PROPOSAL 4

Our 4th proposal included adding 20 solar panels with an additional 2 panels for a solar water heating system. This resulted in the biggest impact to the energy rating which fell from 104 to 24.

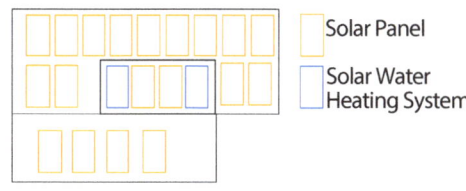

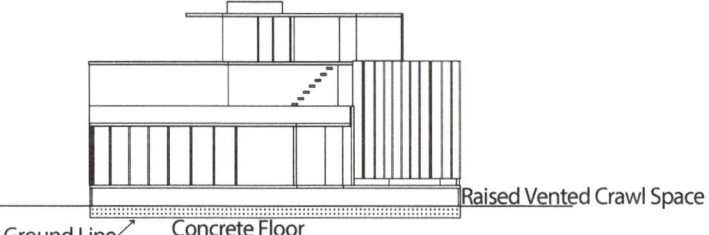

	Energy Cost (Dollars)	Site Energy (kBTU)	Site Energy (kWH)	CO2 Site Production(lbs)	EUI
Original House	$4,924.91	171,168.05	50,166.49	23,211.79	74
Net Zero Proposal	$943.72	-12,342.08	-3,617.26	-2,789.95	-4

PROPOSAL 5

Our fifth proposal included having all the windows and doors be manually opened as well as removing all fans from the house as natural ventilation through the open doors and windows is enough. We also included the best avaliable heat pump as well as extended overhangs. The over hang above the exposed balcony was extended as well as the overhang on the west side of the building. This redced the energy rating from 24 to -13.

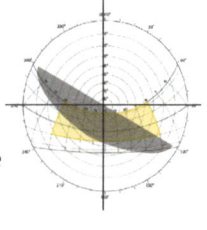
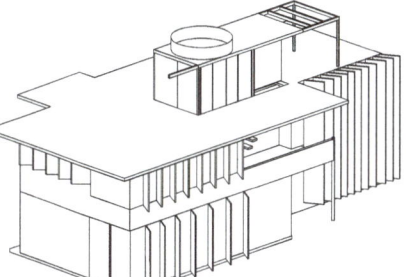

VDL House | City, CA

City, CA | Architect: Richard Neutra
Group 23: Josue Navarro, Hannah Doan, Gabriela Martinez, Ruth Morales, Nayeon Kim

    VDL house is in southern California, which is considered as California Climate Zone 9. And it's characterized to be hot and dry. According to the time table plot, it's depicted that May through October (6months), heat is the main factor. At the end of June and September from 8:30 am to 7:30 pm is when it's excessively heated. Which can be assumed that there will be need for reducing the temperature naturally. In the Sun shading chart, it's shown that the heating is needed in December to Jun from 5am to 9am and shading or cooling is needed from June to December at 11am to 3pm.

    We picked the long window with an overhang as their shade degrees and an HSA of about 1.11. Based on the site where the house is situated, it should be shaded for about 244 hours between June 21 to December 21, for it to reach comfort level. Meanwhile, from December 21 to June 21, there should be shade for about 257 hours to reach comfort cause that is the location of the window between June and December, from 11am to 3pm, because it does its best to keep the heat out, but unfortunately it only shades the window for sixty-percent of the time.

    VDL house has already has overhangs that block direct radiation of summer, but the angle allows sun penetration during the winter. VDL house uses wide openings to bring in indirect natural light reducing the need for artificial light. The house is shadedusing vegetation planted around the house. And prevailing wind from the Silverlake reservoir across the street helps to cool with natural ventilation. The wind pass through the house in the central courtyard between the main house and the Garden house. Thick concrete slab, thermal mass, allows for heat collection during the day which collects solar energy and keep the temperature of the house warm at night From analyzing the psychrometric chart and looking up the 2030 pallet's and climate consultant's recommendations. We could customize the glazing, south window clear to get more natural light in and rest three sides glazed. Another recommendation was to choose materials that has high thermal mass to reduce the temperature fluctuation. The last two was to use natural wind for ventilation. By placing window across from the other opening (door or window) can help the building to have cross ventilation effect which is a very effective way passive cooling. Another way was to have whole house fan so that hot air can effectively escape the building. NZE project Part 2) Summary

    The VDL House existing system includes large windows, overhangs, aluminum sun louvers, large sliding doors, vegetation and a reservoir. Although these devices help bring in sunlight, provide shade and allow natural ventilation, there is still existing problems. For instance, the large windows allow the sunlight to transfer heat into the house, however, there is no current device that creates shade for most of the large windows. Another problem is the thin steel walls allows the heat to escape and the cold to enter during winter. Lastly, there is only one operable sliding door that allows ventilation into the house. In order to fix these problems, we added white opaque interior shades to the large windows to create shade. The shades also l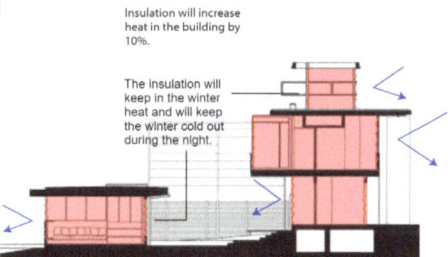crease the temperature of the house. We added insulation to the walls to keep the winter heat inside the house and keep the cold out. By adding 2.0 times the current code value we maximized the heat of the building by 10%. Lastly, to allow more ventilation in the house we added operable windows, fans and air conditioning. The operable windows allow 8% more natural ventilation and the ceiling fans and air condition work as a cooling system.

VDL House - Silver Lake, CA

Architect: Richard Neutra

MEMBERS: HANNAH DOAN, JOSUE NAVARRO, RUTH MORALES, GABBY MARTINEZ, NAYEON KIM

CLIMATE ANALYSIS

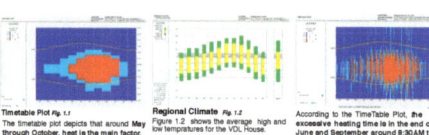

Timetable Plot *Fig. 1.1*
The timetable plot depicts that around May through October, heat is the main factor.

Regional Climate *Fig. 1.2*
Figure 1.2 shows the average high and low temperatures for the VDL House.

According to the TimeTable Plot, the excessive heating time is in the end of June and September around 9:30AM to 7:30PM

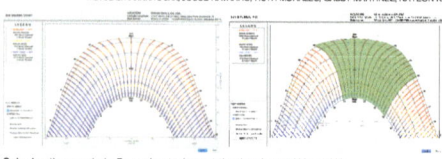

Solar heating needed : December to June at the time from 5AM to 9AM
Shading or cooling needed: June to December at 11AM to 3PM

The VDL house was initially built in 1932 and rebuilt in 1964. The VDL home is designed with the idea of fluidity in mind yet while simultaneously restricting the spaces that are made throughout the home. The home sits in front of the Silver Lake Reservoir. The entire front of the home is covered in window panels that capitalize the view. For its time, it was strong in the design as well as in its materiality. The VDL was considered to be efficient and forward thinking for its time. That is not the case for today's standards. In order to be with the standards of efficiency today, several changes must be made.

Climate file used
California Climate zone 9
City Los Angeles
Coordinates 34.0809, -118.2729
Climate Zone Hot and dry
Distance of VDL to weather file 1.7mi

SHADING ANALYSIS

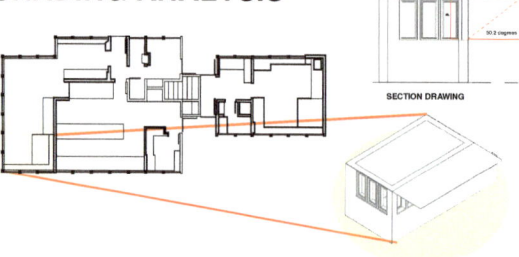

SECTION DRAWING

AXO DRAWING

OP = HP/tan VSA
tanVSA= HP/OP
= 6ft/5ft
=1.2

VSA = arctan(2)
VSA = 50.2 degrees

(6/5) x tan(50) = 1.44
Cos40 = x/1.44
(1.44)Cos40=x
x=1.11
HSA=1.11

SUN PATH DIAGRAM   LATITUDE: 27°N

RECOMMENDED STRATEGIES

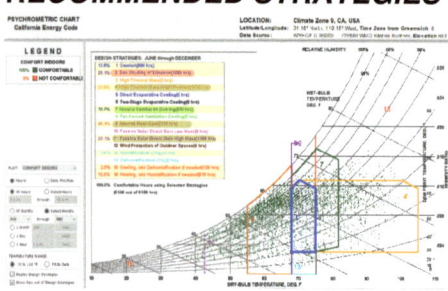

Psychrometric Chart

STRATEGIES FROM 2030 PALETTE

1. CUSTOMIZING THE GLAZING

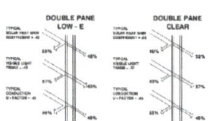

Provide double pane high performance glazing (Low-E) on west, north, and east, but clear on south for maximum passive solar gain

2. CHOOSE MATERIALS WITH HIGH THERMAL MASS

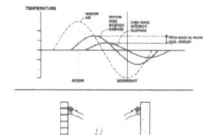

High thermal mass interior surfaces (tile, slate, stone, brick or adobe) feel naturally cool on hot days and can reduce day-to-night temperature swings

3.1 CROSS VENTILATION

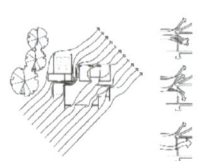

To facilitate cross ventilation, locate door and window openings on opposite sides of building with larger openings facing up-wind if possible

3.2 INSTALLING WHOLE HOUSE FAN

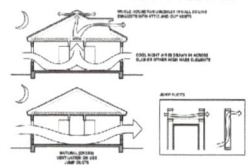

A whole-house fan or natural ventilation can store nighttime 'coolth' in high mass interior surfaces (night flushing), to reduce or eliminate air conditioning

1. SUN SHADING WINDOW

During warm summer months, overhangs block unwanted direct sunlight from solar glazing, reducing cooling loads. Locate an overhang above solar glazing (facing the equator – south in northern latitudes and north in southern latitudes) so it does not block the winter sun.

2. INTERNAL HEAT GAIN

Thermal mass – masonry floors, walls and/or ceilings – absorb and store daytime solar heat in winter for release at night.
A large portion of the sunlight (heat gain) admitted into a space during the daytime must be stored inside the same space for release during the nighttime hours.

3. NATURAL VENTILATION

Buildings can be ventilated and/or cooled by taking advantage of naturally occurring wind currents.
Window openings located perpendicular to prevailing winds, and coupled with openings on the opposite side of a space or building, will provide natural ventilation for fresh air and/or space cooling. Adequate cross ventilation will remove heat from a space or building and maintain indoor air temperatures approximately 1.5 C° (2.7 F°) above the outdoor air temperatures.

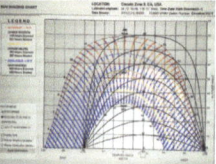

For the VDL house, we picked the long window with an overhang as their shade degrees and an HSA of about 1.11. Based on the site where the house is situated, it should be shaded for about 244 hours between June 21 to December 21, in order for it to reach comfort level. Meanwhile, from December 21 to June 21, there should be shade for about 257 hours to reach comfort cause that is the location of the window between June and December, from 11am to 3pm, because it does its best to keep the heat out, but unfortunately it only shades the window for sixty-percent of the time.

ANALYSIS

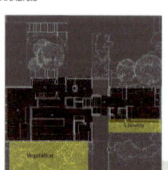

 1 Large Windows

 2 Overhangs

6 Too much sun

5 Vegetation & Reservoir

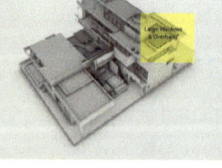

3 Aluminum Sun louvers

4 Large Sliding Door

Existing System
1 Large Windows- placed around the building allows enough light in the house at different times of the days
2 Overhangs- multiple used to provide shade to the large glass walls
3 Aluminum Sun Louvers- added to create shade for the rooms, the be adjusted for different times of the day
4 Large Sliding Door- In common areas on the second floor which allows for natural ventilation through the space
5 Vegetation & Reservoir- plants placed in the front of the building create shade and Silver Lake across the street creates moist ventaliation

Existiing Problems
6 The large windows, although, they are beneficial can also become problematic due to the large amount of sun entering the space.
7 Thin steel walls are allowing the heat and cold through the house

VDL House - Silver Lake, CA

Architect: Richard Neutra

MEMBERS: HANNAH DOAN, JOSUE NAVARRO, RUTH MORALES, GABBY MARTINEZ, NAYEON KIM

VDL

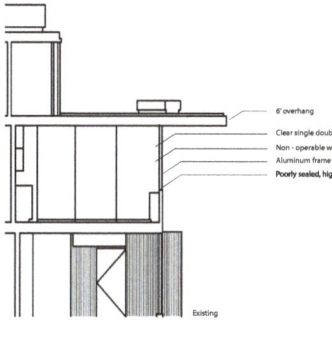

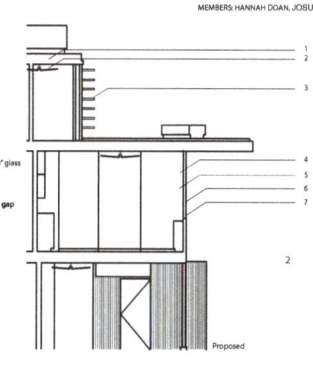

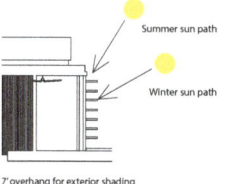
25 KW AC system panels on roof

Ceiling fans with smart thermostat

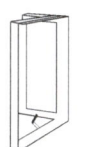
Summer sun path
Winter sun path

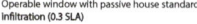
7' overhang for exterior shading

Design Strategy & Proposal

One of the design choices that Nuetra made for the home was to have glass along the East and West facades of the home. It is important to keep in mind Nutras intentions while remodeling the home to attain today's standards of efficiency. To be able to achieve zero-net energy, the windows need to be addressed. Replacing the single paned windows with double paned, argon filled glass will improve the VDL house. In order to continue this journey of achieving a zero-net energy building, there needs to be an improvement with insulation and interior shading along with updating the outdated furnace and HVAC systems. Along with these elements that we will add to achieve efficiency we will add solar panels to the roof of the building.

Keeping the architects design intentions, nothing with removed from the architecture, but we were able to achieve our goal of efficiency by either replacing, upgrading, or adding different elements throughout the VDL house.

Exisitng VDL House

No insulation
Clear single 1/8" glass in aluminum frame
Natural ventilation: Few operable windows
No indoor fans
Heating: No furnace
Cooling: No air conditioner
No operable shading
No PV panels

Proposed Elements

Super insulation: 2.0 times current code value	10%
Clear aron filled DBL pane low E aluminum frame	
Natural ventilation: All operable windows	8%
Smart thermostat ceiling fans	
Heating: No furnace	57%
Cooling: Best available air conditioner	
White opaque interior shades - maximum solar gain	
5 KW AC system - 25 panels	47%

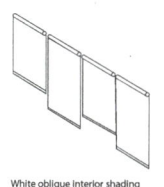
Low E window with Aluminum framing

Operable window with passive house standard
Infiltration (0.3 SLA)

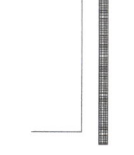
White oblique interior shading

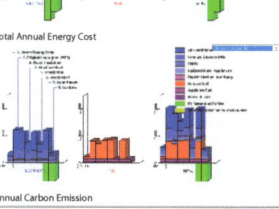
Total Annual Energy Cost

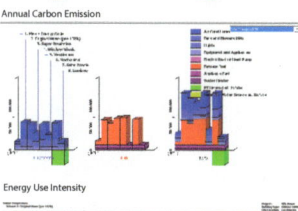
Annual Carbon Emission

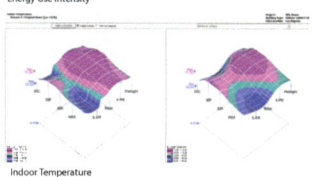
Energy Use Intensity

Indoor Temperature

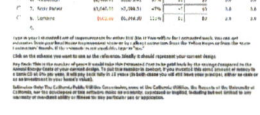
Home Energy Rating

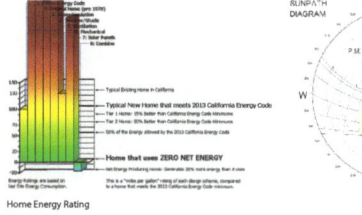

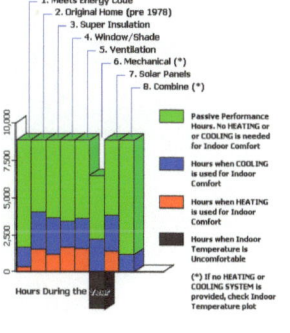
Energy Effective Design

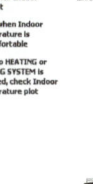

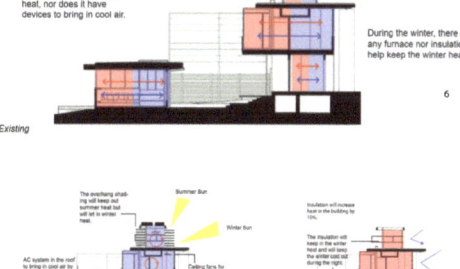

Super Insulation 2x current code

125

Syllabus

Department of Architecture, College of Environmental Design
California State Polytechnic University, Pomona

Arc 331/331-01,02,03,04 Environmental Control Systems I
Spring Semester 2019

INSTRUCTOR
Pablo La Roche, Ph.D.
Office ARC: Building 7, Room 103e   e-mail: pmlaroche@cpp.edu
Office CRS: Building 209 B
Telephone: Office (909) 869-2700   Dept. Secretary (Rocky) (909) 869-2683
Office hours: M   2:00 PM - 4:00 PM
By appointment at other times

COURSE TIMES AND LOCATION
Class/Lecture: ARC 3310-01   F   9:00 - 10:50 AM   @ 66-202

Discussion Sections:
ARC 3312-01   S1 M   10:00 - 10:50 PM   @ 89-1C
ARC 3312-02   S2 M   11:00 - 11:50 PM   @ 89-1D
ARC 3312-03   S3 W   10:00 - 10:50 AM   @ 89-1C
ARC 3312-04   S4 W   11:00 - 11:50 AM   @ 89-1D

TEACHING ASSISTANT
Jake Chevrier   jmchevrier@cpp.edu

1. CATALOG DESCRIPTION
ARC 3310 Environmental Control Systems I (3)
Performance principles and systems to reduce the environmental impact of buildings and to address occupant comfort. Thermal comfort, climate analysis, solar geometry, daylighting, passive heating and cooling, renewable energy and mechanical systems.

2. PREREQUISITES AND COMPONENTS
Prerequisite(s): ARC Graduate Standing and Undergraduate Standing; ARC 201 or ARC 2010; and ARC 201L or ARC 2011L.
Corequisite(s): ARC 3312.
Component(s): One 2-hour lecture, one 1-hour lab

3. COURSE DESCRIPTION
This is the first of a two-course series on environmental controls in buildings. Sustainable architectural design must consider multiple issues such as site, indoor environmental quality, energy, light, materials, and water. An understanding of the concepts of solar geometry, thermal comfort, the effects of climate on the thermal performance of buildings, fundamentals of daylight and electrical lighting, and acoustics, are important for appropriate integration of environmental control systems in buildings. Architects are not required to perform the tasks of mechanical or electrical engineers; however, architects must understand the basic principles to control design outcomes and become team leaders in the making of low carbon architecture.

4. COURSE OBJECTIVES AND LEARNING OUTCOMES
The course work during this quarter will emphasize control systems for the thermal environment and the results of the class will enable the student to:
     1. Understand building related sustainability concepts
     2. Understand the environmental impact of buildings, including their effect on climate change.
     3. Understand the concept of climate sensitive design and the relationship between climate, buildings, thermal comfort and energy use in buildings.
     4. Understand the design issues that affect thermal comfort, energy consumption and other indoor environmental requirements for human occupancy.
     5. Understand passive heating and cooling systems and their application in different climates
     6. Understand mechanical heating and cooling systems for small buildings and their design and layout.
     7. Understand the principles of environmental building systems required to practice architecture in the United States.

The course includes six general topics:

1. Psychrometrics and thermal comfort
2. Site, climate and architecture
3. Solar geometry
4. Energy and buildings, including passive and active cooling and heating systems and renewable energy options.
5. Introduction to mechanical heating and cooling systems
6. Daylight principles

The course will be conducted in both lecture and seminar/lab formats which will involve theory, practical applications, calculations, and appropriate hands-on experiments with performance modeling tools. Topics are explained in lectures, practiced in the labs and integrated in the design process with the Net Zero Energy Project.

5. REFERENCES AND RESOURCES / HARDWARE AND SOFTWARE
Multiple resources will be used in this class, books, websites, and energy modeling software and the class Blackboard site.

REQUIRED TEXTS, RESOURCES & SOFTWARE
1. Carbon Neutral Architectural Design. Pablo La Roche 2nd edition CRC Press, 2017.
2. Course Lectures available through Blackboard site
3. Course Reader available through Blackboard site
4. The Passive Solar Energy Book. Ed Mazria, 1979. Available as a PDF on BB (w permission of the author)

RECOMMENDED TEXTS
The following texts and resources are highly recommended for this class and for future reference
1. Mechanical and Electrical Equipment for Buildings, 12th edition. Stein, Reynolds, Kwok and Grondzik. Wiley, 2014.
2. Heating, Cooling, Lighting: Design Methods for Architects,4th Edition. N. Lechner, published by John Wiley & Sons 2014.
3. Architectural Lighting, Second Edition. M. David Egan, Victor Olgyay. McGraw Hill, 2nd Ed, 2002
4. Simplified Design of Building Lighting (Parker/Ambrose Series of Simplified Design Guides), Schiler, 1992
5. Daylighting and Integrated Lighting Design. Christopher Meek, Kevin Van Den Wymelenberg
6. Daylighting Handbook I, Christoph Reinhart Building Technology Press, 2014.
7. Going to Zero and Going to Zero 2017. These two books include student projects for ARC 3310 and are a helpful reference for your projects.

REQUIRED SOFTWARE
1. Climate Consultant software for Climate Analysis
Available at http://www.energy-design-tools.aud.ucla.edu/climate-consultant/request-climate-consultant.php
2. HEED software for Energy Modeling
Available at http://www.energy-design-tools.aud.ucla.edu/heed/

REQUIRED RESOURCES
1. Tophat will be used in class as an active learning tool
2. AIA+2030 Online Series Course is available for free using the code CALPOLY2030
https://aiau.aia.org/aia2030-online-series download the courses in the series (1,2,3,4,5,6,7,8,10) all except course 9
3. 2030 Palette available at: http://2030palette.org/

ADDITIONAL READINGS
The following texts and resources are also highly recommended for this class and for future reference
1. Simplified Design of HVAC Systems, by W. Bobenhausen, published by Wiley, 2000.
2. Climate Design, by Donald Watson, and Kenneth Lab, published by John Wiley & Sons.
3. Design with Climate, by Victor Olgyay, published by Princeton University Press.
4. Plea Note 6, Keeping Cool: Principles to Avoid Overheating in Buildings. La Roche, P., Quirós, C., Bravo, G., Machado, M., Gonzalez G., (2001). Kangaroo Valley, Australia: Passive Low Energy Architecture Association & Research Consulting and Communications, 60 p.
5. Ecohouse III A Design Guide. Sue Roaf & Manuel Fuentes. Architectural Press, Third edition 2007.
6. Adapting Buildings and Cities for Climate Change, Sue Roaf, David Crichton, Fergus Nicol. Architectural Press, 2005
7. Introduction to Architectural Science: The Basis of Sustainable Design, Steven Szokolay, Elsevier 2004.
8. Climate Considerations in Building and Urban Design, Baruch Givoni 1998.
9. ARE practice software and Books.

10. How Buildings Work, The Natural Order of Architecture. Edward Allen. Oxford University Press, 2nd Ed, 1995.
11. Daylighting Handbook. Christoph Reinhart, 2014

COMMUNICATION
Face to face synchronous communication will be complemented by the use of Blackboard and Top Hat active learning technologies. The Blackboard site will be used to post announcements and will include all lectures, grades and reading materials. Social media will also be used as needed and an option for an extra credit video will be posted online.

6. COURSE REQUIREMENTS AND GRADING
The grading policy for the course is as follows:

1.	Net Zero Energy Project (teams of 4-5)	25%
2.	Quiz	10%
3.	Midterm exam	20%
4.	Final exam	25%
5.	Labs	12%
6.	Class participation (includes course questions)	8%
	Total	100%.

Attendance will be taken at every class, students with more than two unexcused absences will be subject to a lower letter grade. The instructor also holds the right to administratively drop (or to fail) the student if they exceed three unexcused absences.

Net Zero Energy Design Project
A net zero-energy building (NZEB) is a residential or commercial building with greatly reduced energy needs through efficiency gains such that all the energy required can be supplied with renewable technologies. In a NZEB the total amount of energy used by the building on an annual basis is equal to (or less than) the amount of renewable energy created on the site. The California energy code states that by the year 2020 all new residential construction in California has to be net zero energy.

Students will work in teams of five to convert a well-known mid-century California home into a net zero energy and net zero carbon (for operation) house. Several metrics will be used to evaluate building performance, the main ones being Energy Use Intensity (EUI) for energy, and Carbon Emissions measured in carbon dioxide equivalent (CO_2e).

Teams must select one of the twentieth-century Los Angeles homes below. These homes are well known and there are multiple references for them. I have posted several papers in blackboard that implement sustainable studies of some of these houses.

- Case Study House 22 by Pierre Koenig
- VDL house by Richard Neutra
- Eames House by Charles and Ray Eames
- Schrage House by Rafael Soriano
- Ray Kappe Residence by Ray Kappe
- King's Road House by R.M Schindler

Teams should first analyze the home as originally designed and compare its performance with a building as designed under current code. You will then propose design modifications to improve its performance so that the home complies with the NZE requirement of what the California 2020 energy code will be. Proposals must compare modeled energy consumption and carbon emissions of the home as it was originally designed with your proposal, explaining how your design strategies work.

This project must be designed with the graphical quality of an architectural design studio using performance modeling to support design decisions. The process should be clear with results and design ideas clearly explained using your own charts and infographics. No copyrighted images or photographs from other sources should be used. Remember that this is about good design that must perform. Be creative!!! Explore new ideas and demonstrate that they work.
Remember that ALL NZE projects will be included in a book to be published at the end of the semester. It is in your best interest to do a good project. The best NZE projects will be presented in interim and included in the ARC CPP book

GRADING
All courses in Architecture are evaluated for core competencies in, 1) Oral Communication, 2) Critical Thinking, 3) Information Literacy and 4) Quantitative Reasoning. Course projects, papers and presentations will be assessed in each of these categories to determine if a student's work meets Introductory, Developing, or Mastery level outcomes.

- A **Superior Work**
  Indicates originality and independent work and a thorough mastery of the subject matter/skill; achievement so outstanding that it is normally attained only by students doing truly exemplary work.
- B **Very Good Work**
  Indicates clearly better than adequate competence in the subject matter/skill; achievement of quality higher than adequate, but not of exemplary quality.
- C **Adequate Work**
  Indicates that classroom work, outside assignments, and examinations have been completed at a level indicating adequate competence in the subject matter/skill.
- D **Minimally Acceptable Work** (C- and below not acceptable for Graduate contract work)
  Indicates achievement which meets the minimum requirements of the course, but at a level indicating less than adequate competence in the subject matter/skill.
- F **Unacceptable Work**
  Indicates achievement that fails to meet the minimum requirements of the course and is clearly below university quality; not a passing grade.

EXTRA CREDIT
There will be several opportunities for extra credit indicated below.

1) Video
A video that narrates your project development or a concept in the course that has caught your attention.
An example of a previous extra credit video:
https://www.youtube.com/watch?v=vXYayNVhQpg

2) Jump Into STEM
Enroll in the competition and submit your idea for a product that can be used for a residential building wall retrofit intended to replace or supplement current, leaky, and unhealthy walls. This is an opportunity to participate in a STEM competition.
https://jump.ideascale.com/a/index
https://jump.ideascale.com/a/ideas/top/campaign-filter/byids/campaigns/22991/stage/unspecified#link1

3) Volunteer activity at the Lyle Center
You have the opportunity to work on directed activities at the Lyle Center for Regenerative Studies. These include harvesting, planting, cleaning. To reserve a spot and get credit for your work go to the link below. However if you reserve a spot, please honor it. No shows are not helpful for your friends or the center. You should sign up in the link below.
http://signup.com/go/bgWFVOF

3) Report on the AIA 2030 series
Viewing the series in mandatory, and questions will be included in exams and quizzes regarding the videos. Extra credit will be given for a presentation or a video that describes what you have learned in the videos. Extra credit will also be given for a passing all the quizzes. You have until the date of the final exam for this.

7. ACADEMIC POLICIES
University:
Students must adhere to University policies regarding academic integrity (plagiarism), health (drug and alcohol abuse), conduct and discipline and proper relations between students, faculty and staff, including policies on sexual harassment. The policies are contained in the University Catalog, available online. Students are encouraged to familiarize themselves with these policies. All courses within ENV utilize safe practices and strive for students' success within a safe environment. Failure to comply with written safety practices may result in referral to the office of Student Conduct & Integrity (http://www.cpp.edu/~studentconduct/) for Disciplinary Action.

Title IX:
The University is committed to creating and sustaining a positive learning and working environment, free from discrimination, including sexual violence, dating violence, domestic violence and stalking. All forms of such behaviors are not tolerated and are prohibited both by law and university policy. The University will respond promptly to reports of such behavior and will take appropriate action to prevent, correct, and when necessary discipline behavior that violates University policy. If you experience sexual assault, domestic violence, dating violence or stalking, you are encouraged to seek immediate assistance from police, a confidential sexual assault counselor or advocate, and healthcare provider for your physical safety, emotional support and medical care. I encourage you to please review the University's Title IX website for additional information: https://www.cpp.edu/~officeofequity/titleIX/. University policy requires me, as a faculty member, to report any of the above behaviors that are disclosed to me, to the University Title IX Coordinator so that the University may take immediate action to prevent, correct, and/or discipline as appropriate. Given this, please know that if I feel that you are beginning to share information with me concerning sexual assault, domestic violence, dating violence or stalking, I may gently interrupt you to advise you of this and to allow you an opportunity to decide whether you would like to continue to disclose this information to me or whether you would prefer a confidential resource. I care for your physical and emotional health and safety and will do my best to assist you with resources and support, which may include interim accommodations.

Department of Architecture:

The Department of Architecture has established specific policies regarding studio culture and safety. These policies are described on the architecture website.

8. COURSE SCHEDULE

Week	Day	Lecture Topics	Assignments
Week 1			

INTRODUCTION

JAN 21	M	MLK No lab	
JAN 23	W	NO LAB	
JAN 25	F	Lecture 1: Introduction: Climate Change and Architecture Carbon Neutral Architectural Design Chapter 1,2,3,4	
		AIA+2030 Online Series Course 1: The 2030 Challenge: Goals and Design Processes	

SECTION 1: HUMAN THERMAL COMFORT

		Lecture 2: Psychrometrics & Thermal Comfort Software: PMV tool http://cbe.berkeley.edu/comforttool/ Carbon Neutral Design Chapter 5	Introduce NZE Project

Week 2

JAN 28	M (LAB)	Lecture 3: Physiological & Adaptive Comfort Carbon Neutral Design Chapter 5 Software: Climate Consultant	
JAN 30	W (LAB)	Lecture 3: Physiological & Adaptive Comfort Carbon Neutral Design Chapter 5 Software: Climate Consultant	
		AIA+2030 Online Series Course 3: Accentuate the Positive: Climate Responsive Design (sections 3 and 4)	

SECTION 2: CLIMATE AND ARCHITECTURE

| FEB 1 | M | Lecture 4: Climate Responsive Design
Carbon Neutral Design Chapter 6
Software: Climate Consultant | DUE Team members NZE Project |

AIA+2030 Online Series Course 3: Accentuate the Positive: Climate Responsive Design
(all other sections 1,2,5,6,7)

Week 3

| FEB 4 | M | Lab 1: Thermal Comfort and Climate |
| FEB 6 | W | Lab 1: Thermal Comfort and Climate |

SECTION 3: SOLAR GEOMETRY

| FEB 8 | F | Lecture 5: Solar Geometry: The Sun and the Earth
Carbon Neutral Design Chapter 7 |

Lecture 6: Solar Geometry: The Sun and the Buildings
Carbon Neutral Design Chapter 7

Week 4

SECTION 4: ENERGY AND BUILDINGS

| FEB 11 | M | Lab 2: Climate and Solar Geometry | DUE Lab 1: Thermal Comfort |
| FEB 13 | W | Lab 2: Climate and Solar Geometry | |
| FEB 15 | F | Lecture 7: Heat Transfer by Conduction.
Carbon Neutral Design Chapter 8 | QUIZ Sections 1, 2, 3 |

AIA+2030 Online Series Course 4: Building Skin: The Importance of the Thermal Envelope

Week 5

| FEB 18 | M | Individual review w Teams NZE Projects | DUE Lab 2: Solar Geometry |
| FEB 20 | W | Individual review w Teams NZE Projects | |
| FEB 22 | F | Lecture 8: Heat Transfer by Convection and Radiation
Carbon Neutral Design Chapter 8 | |

Lecture 9: Heat Loss Calculations

Week 6

| FEB 25 | M | Individual review w Teams NZE Projects | |
| FEB 27 | W | Individual review w Teams NZE Projects | |
| MAR 1 | M | Lecture 10: Passive Cooling
Carbon Neutral Design Chapter 9 | DUE: NZE Project Part 1 |

AIA+2030 Online Series Course 5: Employing Passive Systems for Load Reduction

Week 7

MAR 4   M   Lab 3: U value calculations

MAR 6   W   Lab 3: U value calculations

MAR 8   F   Lecture 11: Passive Heating
Carbon Neutral Design Chapter 10

Week 8

MAR 11 M   Lab 4: Heat Loss calculations   DUE Lab 3: U value Calculations

MAR 13 W   Lab 4: Heat Loss calculations

MAR 15 W   Lecture 12: Energy Modeling
Carbon Neutral Design Chapter 11

AIA+2030 Online Series Course 2: The Power of Targets and Load Reduction

Week 9

MAR 18 M   Individual review w Teams NZE Projects   DUE Lab 4: Heat Loss Calculations

MAR 20 W   Individual review w Teams NZE Projects

MAR 22 F   MID TERM EXAM

Week 10
MAR 25 M   Individual review w Teams NZE Projects

MAR 27 W   Individual review w Teams NZE Projects

MAR 29 F   Lecture 13: Active Solar: Hot Water & Space Heating
MEEB C 29

Lecture 14: Renewable Energy
MEEB C 9

AIA+2030 Online Series Course 8: The Role of Renewable Energy

SPRING BREAK

APR 1   M   SPRING BREAK
APR 3   W   SPRING BREAK
APR 5   F   SPRING BREAK

Week 11

APR 8   M   Individual review w Teams NZE Projects

APR 10 W   Individual review w Teams NZE Projects

SECTION 5: MECHANICAL SYSTEMS

APR 12	F	Lecture 15: Mechanical Heating in Small Buildings MEEB C 9	DUE: NZE Project Part 2
		Lecture 16: Mechanical Cooling in Small Buildings MEEB C 9	
		AIA+2030 Online Series Course 7: High Performance Building Systems	

Week 12

APR 15	M	Individual review w Teams NZE Projects
APR 17	W	Individual review w Teams NZE Projects
APR 19	F	Guest Lecture on Sustainable Engineering Brian Berg, GLUMAC
		AIA+2030 Course 10: Putting it Together: Achieving 2030 Goals on the Project and in the Office (optional)

Week 13

APR 22	M	Individual review w Teams NZE Projects
APR 24	W	Individual review w Teams NZE Projects

SECTION 6: INTRODUCTION TO LIGHT

APR 26	F	Lecture 17: Light, Basic Concepts I Egan & Olgyay; Schiler, Reinhart, MEEB C 11	
		Lecture 18: Light, Basic Concepts II Egan & Olgyay; Schiler, Reinhart, MEEB C 11	Due NZE Project Final
		AIA+2030 Online Series Course 6: Daylighting and Integrated Lighting Design	

Week 14

APR 29	M	NZE Project Presentations
MAY 1	W	NZE Project Presentations
MAY 3	F	Lecture 19: Visual Task Egan & Olgyay; Schiler, Reinhart, MEEB C 11
		Lecture 20: Design w Daylight Software: DIVA & Daylight Calculations Egan & Olgyay; Schiler, Reinhart, MEEB C 12

Week 15

MAY 6   M   No Section

MAY 8   W   No Section

MAY 10 F   Review for Final Exam   Extra Credit Presentations

Finals Week (May 11-19)

FINAL EXAM DATE DETERMINED BY UNIVERSITY

NOTE: Students are advised to refer to the university catalog for dates and procedures on incomplete and/or course withdrawal. No make-up tests for mid-term or final examination will be given without a written medical excuse and permission from the instructor. Also refer to the university catalog on copyrights, plagiarism, and student codes of conduct. Check in Blackboard frequently for new information and updates.

Net Zero Energy Project

ARC 3310: Environmental Control Systems Prof. Pablo La Roche
California State Polytechnic University Pomona

Assigned: January 25
Team list due February 1
Part I due MARCH 1
Part II due APRIL 12
Final Project due APRIL 26

1. INTRODUCTION

Buildings have a significant impact on energy use and the environment. Commercial and residential buildings use almost 40% of the primary energy and approximately 70% of the electricity in the United States (EIA 2005).

A net zero-energy building (NZEB) is a residential or commercial building with greatly reduced energy needs through efficiency gains such that the energy needed can be supplied with renewable technologies. There are several definitions for net zero energy, for this project we will assume that a net-zero energy building will have zero net energy consumption, which means that the total amount of energy used by the building on an annual basis is equal to (or less than) the amount of renewable energy created on the site. It is important to know how to design net zero energy buildings. By the year 2020 all new residential construction in California has to be net zero energy and all new commercial buildings have to be net zero energy by 2030.

Architects and engineers must work together to achieve this goal. Architects usually have responsibility in the design of the envelope (form and materials) while mechanical engineers have more responsibility in the mechanical systems that cool and heat the building. True sustainable and integrated design is achievable working together. This project emphasizes your role as "designers" of buildings that provide comfort with minimum use of energy. The main metric to evaluate building performance will be Energy Use Intensity (EUI).

2. ASSIGNMENT

You will work in teams of four and select one of several well-known mid-century California homes, analyze it and then convert it into a net zero energy building, which will also be low carbon. You will select one of the following twentieth-century iconic Los Angeles homes:

1. Case Study house 22 by P Koenig
2. VDL house by Neutra
3. Eames house by Eames
4. Ray Kappe house
5. King's Road house by R.M Schindler

3. LEARNING OBJECTIVES

After finalizing this exercise you should be able to:

a) Understand the effects of the main climatic factors on building thermal performance.
b) Design a building adapted to climate
c) Determine the impact of form and orientation in energy use and emissions.
d) Determine the impact of WWR in energy use and emissions.
e) Determine the impact of shading in energy use and emissions.
f) Determine the impact of building materials & strategies in energy use and emissions.
g) Determine the most effective design strategies for residential buildings for selected climates.
h) Design a building that is net zero energy. Your design objectives are to:

Minimize Energy Use. Your building should be net zero energy.
Minimize CO_2 emissions. Your building should be net zero carbon for operation

4.   PROCESS & TOOLS

You must first analyze the home in its current state and compare with a current code compliant building. You will then make all necessary modifications to improve its performance and go beyond code to achieve net zero energy.

You will use a climate analysis tool and an energy modeling software for this project.

- Climate Analysis Tool: Climate Consultant
http://www.energy-design-tools.aud.ucla.edu/climate-consultant/request-climate- consultant.php
- HEED. Available from UCLA website through a special link for the class. There are three links for Windows 32 bit, Windows 64 bit, and Mac.

http://www.energy-design-tools.aud.ucla.edu/heed-alpha/request.php

This is the link to the main the main Energy Design Tools site for the full selection of background technical information, tutorials, etc.

http://www.energy-design-tools.aud.ucla.edu/

5.   SUBMISSIONS

5.1.   PART ONE: CLIMATE AND BUILDING ANALYSIS
DUE MARCH 1
FORMAT: 24 x 24

a)   Climate analysis. This climate analysis is for the building at this specific location. Map or diagram indicating site, location of the climate file used, climate zone, distance of site to weather file and additional microclimate information that could affect data from climate file. Explain the climate through the main climate variables, temperature, relative humidity and solar radiation (screen shots from Climate Consultant). Add explicative texts to the screenshots.

Minimum deliverables are:
- Map indicating distance of weather station to house (climate zone)
- Temperature range,
- Timetable plot,

b)   Define overheated and under heated periods using timetable plot diagram from Climate Consultant. You can also use the temperature range chart to compare data. Remember, shade will be needed during the overheated period and sun will be needed during the under heated period.

Minimum deliverables are:
- Timetable plot image with overheated and underheated periods
- Hours and Dates during which shade is needed
- Hours and Dates during which sun is needed

c)   Existing Shade. Determine the performance of at least one shade systemin the house (fin or overhang). Use photograhs, diagrams, calculations and sun path diagrams and shadow masks. Calculate existing VSA and HSA and indicate the shaded period of the year. You should use the method and equations outlined in Carbon Neutral Design, using either a horizontal path diagram or a vertical sun path diagram from Climate Consultant. Concisely explain with diagrams and images.

Minimum deliverables are:
- Diagram, section, or elevation indicating the relationship of the shade with the window.
- Sun Path Diagram with existing Shadow Mask. Indicate VSA and HSA

d) Determine the main bioclimatic strategies for this climate (include examples). Use Climate Consultant's Psychrometric Chart to determine strategies and then use the 2030 palette to select concepts and case studies. Remember that you can link to the 2030 palette from climate consultant. http://2030palette.org/

Minimum deliverables are:
- Psychrometric Chart with selected bioclimatic strategies
- Bullet list of recommended Strategies
- Examples from 2030 Palette

e) Discuss how the house you are analyzing responds to climate. Describe in one diagram the main climate responsive design guidelines in the home that you are analyzing. It is recommended that you look at site design, building layout and massing, building envelope, shading and sun control, wind control, indoor layout, EUI. Determine what works and what doesn't work. You will indicate all of this in a sustainability diagram.

Minimum deliverables are:
- Sustainability diagram indicating sustainable strategies
- Estimated values of SHGC, U value, VLT of windows and R values of walls.

f) Description of Sustainable Strategies in house. Describe sustainable design and climate responsive features in your house. This is a separate document in 100 words

Minimum deliverables are:
- 100-word text file

5.2. PART TWO: DESIGN PROPOSAL
DUE APRIL 12
FORMAT: 24 x 24

Develop a design incorporating your proposals to improve performance and achieve net zero energy. You will use energy modeling with HEED for this portion of the project.

a) Propose improvement in shade system analyzed in part one. Determine the performance of improvements for at least one shade system in the house (fin or overhang).

Minimum deliverables are:
- Diagram, section, or elevation indicating the relationship of the shade proposal with the window.
- Sun Path Diagram with proposed Shadow Mask. Indicate new VSA and HSA

b) Propose appropriate climate responsive strategies to improve building performance. Indicate design strategies and methods that could improve the performance. These strategies are not generic and are specific to the building. Potential strategies include adding insulation in the walls, changing to higher performing windows, adding shade, additional overhangs to improve shade and adding windows for daylight, skylights, planters, PV panels, or passive and active heating or cooling systems. These design modifications should still maintain the spirit of the original design. Use technical drawings, diagrams, sections, perspectives, renderings as required. Include data such as U value and SHGC. Indicate building changes in these drawings.

Minimum deliverables are:
- Proposed strategies
- Proposed values of elements that have changed (eg SHGC, U value, VLT of windows and R values of walls).
- Representative cross section of a wall with U value including calculation. If you added insulation to the wall you should show here

c) Performance Metrics. You should use HEED to analyze the original state and after design modifications. You should include the minimum metrics below. You can plot the data taken from HEED or use screen shots. Use your own spreadsheet and charts as needed.

Minimum deliverables are:
- Total annual energy consumption (kBtu)
- Total annual energy cost in dollars
- Energy Use Intensity EUI
- Annual Carbon Emissions
- One 3d chart

You can add other values such as:
- Annual heating energy and heating $
- Annual cooling energy and cooling $
- Additional 3d charts

Some of the information can be taken from the following HEED screens:
- Home Energy Rating screen (hover above bar chart to get kWh/year and EUI as kBTU/sf for any scheme
- Energy Cost bar charts screens for kBTU, kWh and CO_2 emissions.

d) Sustainable concept diagram. Describe in one sustainability diagram the main climate responsive design guidelines that you are proposing for your home. It is recommended that you look at site design, building layout and massing, building envelope, shading and sun control, wind control, indoor layout, EUI. The diagram should explain the strategies you have implemented in your project to achieve higher performance and net zero energy. It is helpful to show how your building works in the summer and winter and day and night. Include performance data.

Minimum deliverables are:
- Sustainability diagram indicating sustainable strategies
- Proposed values of SHGC, U value, VLT of windows and R values of walls.

f) Description of Proposed Sustainable Strategies in house. Describe the main sustainable design and climate responsive proposed in your house and how they compare to initial performance. Use metrics as appropriate. This is a separate word file

5.3. FINAL SUBMISSION
DUE APRIL 26
Format: Two Boards 24 by 24 inches.

Design a graphically appealing bard. Use analysis to support design decisions. Be sure that your story is clear and that process, results and design are all connected. Create your own charts and infographics. Remember that this is also about design. It is not just technical. It is good design that must perform. Be creative!!! Explore new ideas and demonstrate that they work. You can also incorporate new design features such as a solar wall or a wind scoop.

CONTENT.
- Part one and part two organized in two boards.

NOTES:
- Do not use text with a font smaller than 30 points in the boards.
- The text will be a separate word file with 200 words
- At the end of the course teams will submit a high res PDF of the board, the text and some of the images.

6. GRADING

Grading will be based on fulfilling design objectives and explanation of design strategies.

Climate analysis   20%
Building analysis 40%
Building proposal 40%

7. REFERENCES

These homes are well known and there are multiple references for them. The following papers that I have posted on blackboard can give you some suggestions regarding analysis.

La Roche P., (2001). "A Sustainable Modernist House in Los Angeles: Case Study House 22", Proc. of the Conference of the American Solar Energy Society, Washington DC.

La Roche, (2002), "The Case Study House Program in Los Angeles: A Case for Sustainability", Proc. of PLEA 2002 Conference (Passive and Low Energy Architecture), Toulouse, France.

La Roche, P. Almodóvar J (2009) El Case Study House Program en Los Angeles: Un ejemplo de Sostenibilidad. "Revista de Historia y Teoría de la Arquitectura" nº 8-9. Funded by the Consejería de Cultura de la Junta de Andalucía. ISSN: 1576-5628

La Roche, P., Naversen, L, Jamison M, (2013) Learning Sustainable Design from the Recent Past Mid Twentieth Century Southern California Houses. PLEA 2013 Annual Conference of the Passive Low Energy Association, Munich, Germany.

Carmen Alonso, Pablo La Roche & Ignacio Oteiza (2016): Occupants and energy performance: the Schrage House, Architectural Science Review, DOI: 10.1080/00038628.2016.1205472

YouTube tutorials: https://www.youtube.com/watch?v=znoMYDq5T8Y>View HEED Overview Tutorial (~20 min.)
https://www.youtube.com/watch?v=kFhC821aXU8>View HEED Basic Design Tutorial (~30 min.)
https://www.youtube.com/watch?v=g-pdhm3rClk>View HEED Advanced Design Tutorial (~37 min.). https://www.youTube.com/watch?v=7pxpmdZptDM>View Climate Consultant Overview Tutorial (~10 min.)